1st EDITION

Perspectives on Diseases and Disorders

Cancer

Tom and Gena Metcalf
Editors

616.994
CAN

Detroit • New York • San Francisco • New Haven, Conn. • Waterville, Maine • London

© 2008 Thomson Gale, a part of The Thomson Corporation.

Thomson and Star Logo are trademarks and Gale and Greenhaven Press are registered trademarks used herein under license.

For more information, contact:
Greenhaven Press
27500 Drake Rd.
Farmington Hills, MI 48331-3535
Or you can visit our Internet site at http://www.gale.com

ALL RIGHTS RESERVED.
No part of this work covered by the copyright hereon may be reproduced or used in any form or by any means—graphic, electronic, or mechanical, including photocopying, recording, taping, Web distribution, or information storage retrieval systems—without the written permission of the publisher.

Every effort has been made to trace the owners of copyrighted material.

Cover photo: © Lester V. Bergman/CORBIS

LIBRARY OF CONGRESS CATALOGING-IN-PUBLICATION DATA

Cancer / Tom and Gena Metcalf, book editors.
    p. cm. — (Perspectives on diseases and disorders)
Includes bibliographical references and index.
ISBN-13: 978-0-7377-3870-4 (hardcover)
1. Cancer I. Metcalf, Tom. II. Metcalf, Gena.
RC261C262 2008
616.99'4—dc22   2007035762

ISBN-10: 0-7377-3870-7

Printed in the United States of America

CONTENTS

Introduction   7

CHAPTER 1   Understanding Cancer

1. Cancer Overview   12

   Rosalyn Carson-DeWitt and Teresa G. Odle

   Cancer is a group of almost one hundred diseases that cause uncontrolled cell growth. Cancers have been linked to family history, diet, pollution, infectious agents, tobacco, and other causes.

2. Cancer Among Young People: A Growing Trend   20

   Katherine Hobson

   People between the ages of fifteen and thirty-nine get cancer, but the medical community has been behind in treating young adults. Now hospitals are beginning to address the problem.

3. Recent Advancement in Breast Cancer Research   27

   Reuters Limited

   The discovery of a common breast cancer susceptibility gene is a promising advancement.

4. Gene Therapy May Hold the Key to a Cancer Cure   32

   Ingrid Wickelgren

   DNA therapy offers new and exciting ways to treat even the deadliest forms of cancer.

5. A New Drug Attacks Only Cancer Cells   38

   Andy Coghlan

   Scientists at the University of Alberta report the
   development of a new drug that will kill cancer
   cells.

6. Prostate Cancer: The Most Commonly   42
   Diagnosed Cancer in Men

   Tedd Mitchell

   Early diagnosis along with new methods of prevention and treatment offer hope for the future.

CHAPTER 2   Controversies in Cancer Treatment

1. Secondhand Smoke Causes Cancer   48

   Richard H. Carmona

   No safe level for exposure to secondhand smoke
   exists, and millions of Americans are still exposed
   to it.

2. Secondhand Smoke May Not Cause   55
   Cancer

   James E. Enstrom and Geoffrey C. Kabat

   Controversy remains about the danger of secondhand smoke, which may not be responsible for lung
   cancer and heart disease.

3. A Vaccine Offers Protection Against   64
   Cervical Cancer

   Barbara A. Bledrzycki

   Preteen girls should be required to take a highly
   effective vaccine against the virus that causes
   cervical cancer.

4. A Cervical Cancer Vaccine Poses   **70**
   Problems to Some

   Maryann Napoli

   Girls should not be required to take the cervical cancer vaccine until issues about clinical testing and possible side effects are resolved.

5. Alternative Treatments for Cancer Work   **76**

   Kerry Hughes

   Supplements made from natural compounds show effectiveness in fighting cancer.

6. Alternative Treatments for Cancer Do   **84**
   Not Work

   Ben Goldacre

   There is no truth to the claims from the alternative treatment industry that supplements are effective in fighting cancer.

7. Marijuana Can Ease the Side Effects   **89**
   of Chemotherapy

   The Economist

   Even though marijuana smoke contains tar, cyanide, and carbon monoxide, its medical benefits have been demonstrated to reduce pain, stimulate appetite, and suppress vomiting. It should be available to patients undergoing chemotherapy.

8. Marijuana Has No Medical Application   **96**

   David Evans

   According to the Food and Drug Administration, marijuana is not only subject to abuse, it has no proven medical effectiveness.

CHAPTER 3 Personal Perspectives on Cancer

1. A Theater Director Confronts Throat   102
   Cancer

   John Dillon

   A theater director recounts his experience dealing
   with stage-four—very advanced—throat cancer
   and his life as a survivor.

2. Cancer Myths and Truths   109

   *Caroline Bollinger, Sharon Liao, Maura Kelly,
   Julie D. Blumenfeld, and Amy Kamensky*

   Sixteen cancer survivors share insights into cancer
   treatment and survival.

3. A Swimmer Fights Lung Cancer to the End   115

   P.H. Mullen

   Dying from lung cancer, Jon Steiner competes
   in the Masters World Championship, swimming
   the anchor leg of the men's 200-meter relay.

Glossary   119
Chronology   122
Organizations to Contact   125
For Further Reading   129
Index   133

INTRODUCTION

The causes of cancer are myriad, but one fact stands out: Cancer affects more people over the age of sixty-five. The National Cancer Institute has found that people over the age of sixty-five are ten times more likely to contract cancer and fifteen times more likely to die from it. They account for 60 percent of newly diagnosed cases of cancer and 70 percent of all cancer-related deaths. Males have a greater likelihood of having cancer (one out of two) compared to females (one out of three). These numbers are sobering. By the year 2030 about 20 percent of the U.S. population will be over sixty-five, and the number of people over the age of eighty is projected to increase from 4.3 million to 8.9 million. Consequently, the medical community is intensifying its study of the relationship between age and cancer.

Scientists' opinions differ over how the age factor relates to cancer. Lifestyle choices, environmental factors, diet, and genetic predisposition all play a role in the onset of cancer. Yet, the effects of many of these are not felt until years have passed.

For example, many people use tanning salons even though exposure to ultraviolet radiation increases the risk of melanoma, a particularly deadly cancer of the skin. Similarly, smoking is known to increase the risk of lung and other cancers, yet people continue to engage in the habit. The use of alcohol with smoking compounds the risk of cancer. These lifestyle choices may very well be the factor responsible for a person over the age of sixty-five developing cancer.

Some explanations for the rising rate of cancer among older people are straightforward. The most obvious

Four-year-old Matthew Bentley giggles during a news conference at Hasbro Children's Hospital in Providence, Rhode Island. Some of the doctors who treated his brain tumor sit behind him. (**AP Images**)

are delays in diagnosis and treatment. The elderly may not be screened as frequently or as carefully as younger people. Many elderly people may suffer from misinformation about medical care. Some still regard cancer as a death warrant and do not seek the care that is available to them. The presence of cancer may be masked by other conditions or just by human frailty. Doctors, for example, may not be aggressive in diagnosing cancer, recogniz-

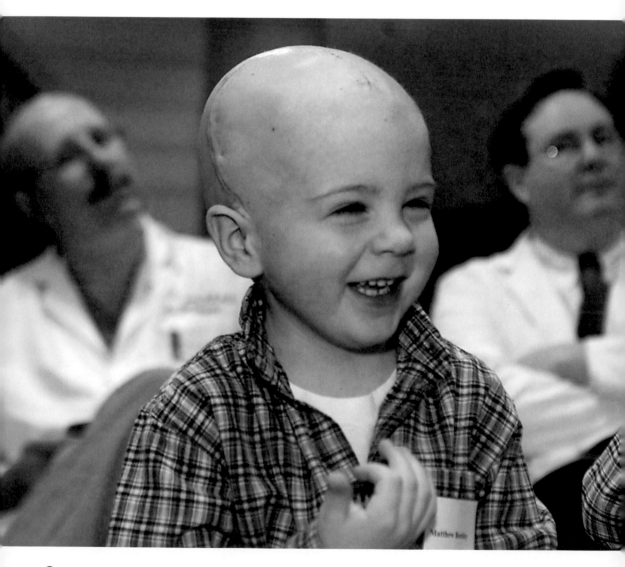

ing that their patients may lack the stamina for tests or treatments.

The relationship between cancer and aging is not precisely understood, however. The elderly have a disproportionately greater mortality rate for the cancers they incur than do their younger counterparts. The medical community is unsure whether cancer among the elderly is due to age (chronological years) or due to aging (exposure to carcinogens during those years). Damage done by oxygen free radicals over the years can have a cumulative effect, and the greater the exposure to carcinogens the faster the aging process is for the body's cells.

Scientists are looking at other aspects of the causes of cancer. Scientists at Baylor University in Houston, for example, have discovered a gene that fights cancer. This gene inhibits the growth of cancerous cells but also has the effect of shortening life. Through experiments with mutant mice with high levels of this gene, researchers found that the cancer-resistant mice had significantly shorter lives. Apparently, the gene not only prevented cancerous growths—it also inhibited the growth of stem cells needed for organs to remain healthy.

Other studies have revealed a curious phenomenon about cancer mortality rates and aging. While the incidence of cancer begins to increase around age forty and accelerates more rapidly for those over sixty-five, it does not continue indefinitely. Cancer-related mortality peaks for people between the ages of eighty and ninety-four and then declines. Thus the extremely elderly are less likely to die of cancer than some other chronic ailment such as heart failure or diabetes. Scientists differ as to the cause.

Some view this anomaly as a statistical reporting problem. The very elderly may die from other chronic ailments even as they are experiencing the onset of cancer. Other researchers, however, who look to environmental factors think that the very elderly may have a reduced incidence of cancer because they have been removed from the environmental factors that cause cancer. By living more sheltered lives, they are less likely to be exposed to environmental causes.

Scientists continue to explore these relationships as well as many other aspects of cancer. One thing is certain about life: The body's cells are programmed to age and die. By studying the causes of disease, scientists come closer to understanding the processes of aging.

CHAPTER 1

Understanding Cancer

Cancer Overview

Rosalyn Carson-DeWitt and Teresa G. Odle

In the following overview, the authors broadly define the characteristics of cancer. They discuss how cancer spreads, its causes, as well as prevention and common treatment. The authors offer guidelines to reduce cancer risk at any age.

Rosalyn Carson-DeWitt is a medical writer who lives in North Carolina. Teresa G. Odle is a writer and editor who has worked in health care communication for many years and is a member of the American Medical Writers Association.

Photo on previous page. At the end of the 2003 Avon Walk for Breast Cancer in Boston, walkers hold pink bandanas in recognition of the fact that during the time it took to complete the walk, 660 women were diagnosed with breast cancer. (AP Images)

Cancer is not just one disease, but a large group of almost 100 diseases. Its two main characteristics are uncontrolled growth of the cells in the human body and the ability of these cells to migrate from the original site and spread to distant sites. If the spread is not controlled, cancer can result in death.

SOURCE: Rosalyn Carson-DeWitt and Teresa G. Odle, from *Gale Encyclopedia of Medicine*, 3rd Edition, Thomson Gale, 2006. Reproduced by permission of Thomson Gale.

One out of every four deaths in the United States is from cancer. It is second only to heart disease as a cause of death in the states. About 1.2 million Americans are diagnosed with cancer annually; more than 500,000 die of cancer annually.

Cancer can attack anyone. Since the occurrence of cancer increases as individuals age, most of the cases are seen in adults, middle-aged or older. Sixty percent of all cancers are diagnosed in people who are older than 65 years of age. The most common cancers are skin cancer, lung cancer, colon cancer, breast cancer (in women), and prostate cancer (in men). In addition, cancer of the kidneys, ovaries, uterus, pancreas, bladder, rectum, and blood and lymph node cancer (leukemias and lymphomas) are also included among the 12 major cancers that affect most Americans.

Mutated Cells Grow Uncontrollably

Cancer, by definition, is a disease of the genes. A gene is a small part of DNA, which is the master molecule of the cell. Genes make "proteins," which are the ultimate workhorses of the cells. It is these proteins that allow our bodies to carry out all the many processes that permit us to breathe, think, move, etc.

Throughout people's lives, the cells in their bodies are growing, dividing, and replacing themselves. Many genes produce proteins that are involved in controlling the processes of cell growth and division. An alteration (mutation) to the DNA molecule can disrupt the genes and produce faulty proteins. This causes the cell to become abnormal and lose its restraints on growth. The abnormal cell begins to divide uncontrollably and eventually forms a new growth known as a "tumor" or neoplasm (medical term for cancer meaning "new growth").

In a healthy individual, the immune system can recognize the neoplastic cells and destroy them before they get a chance to divide. However, some mutant cells may

Frequency of Cancer-Related Death

Cancer Type	Number of Deaths Per Year
Lung	160,100
Colon and rectum	56,500
Breast	43,900
Prostate	39,200
Pancreas	28,900
Lymphoma	26,300
Leukemia	21,600
Brain	17,400
Stomach	13,700
Liver	13,000
Esophagus	11,900
Bladder	12,500
Kidney	11,600
Multiple myeloma	11,300

Source: Rosalyn Carson-DeWitt and Teresa G. Odle in *Gale Encyclopedia of Medicine*, 3rd ed., 2006.

escape immune detection and survive to become tumors or cancers.

Tumors are of two types, benign or malignant. A benign tumor is not considered cancer. It is slow growing, does not spread or invade surrounding tissue, and once it is removed, doesn't usually recur. A malignant tumor, on the other hand, is cancer. It invades surrounding tissue and spreads to other parts of the body. If the cancer cells have spread to the surrounding tissues, even after the malignant tumor is removed, it generally recurs.

A majority of cancers are caused by changes in the cell's DNA because of damage due to the environment. Environmental factors that are responsible for causing the initial mutation in the DNA are called carcinogens, and there are many types. There are some cancers that have a genetic basis. In other words, an individual could inherit faulty DNA from his parents, which could predispose him to getting cancer. While there is scientific evidence that both factors (environmental and genetic) play a role, less than 10% of all cancers are purely hereditary. Cancers that are known to have a hereditary link are breast cancer, colon cancer, ovarian cancer, and uterine cancer. Besides genes, certain physiological traits could be inherited and could contribute to cancers. For example, inheriting fair skin makes a person more likely to develop skin cancer, but only if he or she also has prolonged exposure to intensive sunlight. There are several different types of cancers:

- Carcinomas are cancers that arise in the epithelium (the layer of cells covering the body's surface and lining the internal organs and various glands). Ninety percent of human cancers fall into this category. Carcinomas can be subdivided into two types: adenocarcinomas and squamous cell carcinomas. Adenocarcinomas are cancers that develop in an organ or a gland, while squamous cell carcinomas refer to cancers that originate in the skin.
- Melanomas also originate in the skin, usually in the pigment cells (melanocytes).
- Sarcomas are cancers of the supporting tissues of the body, such as bone, muscle and blood vessels.
- Cancers of the blood and lymph glands are called leukemias and lymphomas respectively.
- Gliomas are cancers of the nerve tissue.

Risk Factors and Warning Signs

The major risk factors for cancer are: tobacco, alcohol, diet, sexual and reproductive behavior, infectious agents, family history, occupation, environment and pollution.

According to estimates of the American Cancer Society (ACS), approximately 40% of cancer deaths in 1998 were due to tobacco and excessive alcohol use. An additional one-third of the deaths were related to diet and nutrition. Many of the one million skin cancers diagnosed in 1998 were due to over-exposure to ultraviolet light from the sun's rays. . . .

Despite the fact that there are several hundred different types of cancers, producing very different symptoms, the ACS has established the following seven symptoms as possible warning signals of cancer:

- changes in the size, color, or shape of a wart or a mole
- a sore that does not heal
- persistent cough, hoarseness, or sore throat
- a lump or thickening in the breast or elsewhere
- unusual bleeding or discharge
- chronic indigestion or difficulty in swallowing
- any change in bowel or bladder habits

Many other diseases, besides cancer, could produce the same symptoms. However, it is important to have these symptoms checked, as soon as possible, especially if they linger. The earlier a cancer is diagnosed and treated, the better the chance of it being cured. Many cancers such as breast cancer may not have any early symptoms. Therefore, it is important to undergo routine screening tests such as breast self-exams and mammograms.

Detection and Treatment Are Essential

Diagnosis begins with a thorough physical examination and a complete medical history. The doctor will observe, feel and palpate (apply pressure by touch) different parts of the body in order to identify any variations from the normal size, feel, and texture of the organ or tissue. . . .

Treatment and prevention of cancers continue to be the focus of a great deal of research. In 2003, research into new cancer therapies included cancer-targeting gene therapy, virus therapy, and a drug that stimulated apoptosis, or self-destruction of cancer cells, but not healthy cells. However, all of these new therapies take years of clinical testing and research.

The aim of cancer treatment is to remove all or as much of the tumor as possible and to prevent the recurrence or spread of the primary tumor. While devising a treatment plan for cancer, the likelihood of curing the cancer has to be weighed against the side effects of the

A cancer patient prepares for radiation therapy. A diagram on his skin indicates the area where he will be treated. **(AP Images)**

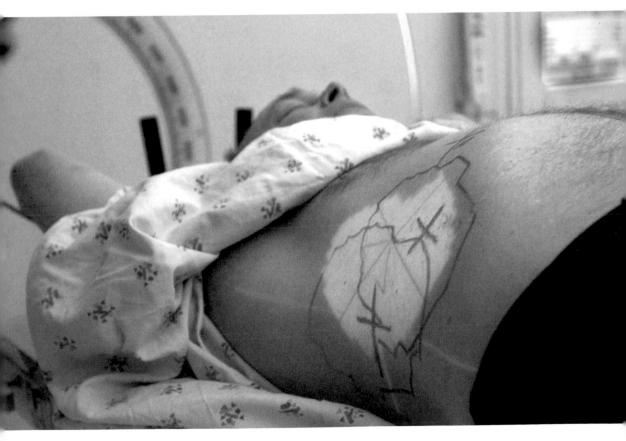

treatment. If the cancer is very aggressive and a cure is not possible, then the treatment should be aimed at relieving the symptoms and controlling the cancer for as long as possible.

Cancer treatment can take many different forms, and it is always tailored to the individual patient. The decision on which type of treatment is the most appropriate depends on the type and location of cancer, the extent to which it has already spread, the patient's age, sex, general health status and personal treatment preferences. The major types of treatment are: surgery, radiation, chemotherapy, immunotherapy, hormone therapy, and bone-marrow transplantation. . . .

FAST FACT

The World Health Organization estimates that of 58 million deaths worldwide in 2005, 13 percent were caused by cancer.

"Lifetime risk" is the term that cancer researchers use to refer to the probability that an individual over the course of a lifetime will develop cancer or die from it. In the United States, men have a one in two lifetime risk of developing cancer, and for women the risk is one in three. Overall, African Americans are more likely to develop cancer than whites. African Americans are also 30% more likely to die of cancer than whites.

Most cancers are curable if detected and treated at their early stages. A cancer patient's prognosis is affected by many factors, particularly the type of cancer the patient has, the stage of the cancer, the extent to which it has metastasized and the aggressiveness of the cancer. In addition, the patient's age, general health status and the effectiveness of the treatment being pursued also are important factors.

To help predict the future course and outcome of the disease and the likelihood of recovery from the disease, doctors often use statistics. The five-year survival rates are the most common measures used. The number refers to the proportion of people with cancer who are expected to be alive, five years after initial diagnosis, compared with a similar population that is free of cancer. It is important to note that while statistics can give some information about the average survival experience of cancer patients in a given population, it cannot be used to indicate individual prognosis, because no two patients are exactly alike.

Prevention

According to nutritionists and epidemiologists from leading universities in the United States, a person can reduce the chances of getting cancer by following some simple guidelines:

- eating plenty of vegetables and fruits
- exercising vigorously for at least 20 minutes every day
- avoiding excessive weight gain
- avoiding tobacco (even second hand smoke)
- decreasing or avoiding consumption of animal fats and red meats
- avoiding excessive amounts of alcohol
- avoiding the midday sun (between 11 A.M. and 3 P.M.) when the sun's rays are the strongest
- avoiding risky sexual practices
- avoiding known carcinogens in the environment or work place

Cancer Among Young People: A Growing Trend

Katherine Hobson

Cancer can strike at any age. That is the message in the following article by Katherine Hobson, a senior editor with *U.S. News & World Report*. Hobson writes that about seventy thousand people between the ages of fifteen and thirty-nine are diagnosed with cancer each year in the United States. Hobson describes how the National Cancer Institute and the Lance Armstrong Foundation are working together to improve the care for this age group. Hobson also considers the problems unique to young adults with cancer. She concludes that conditions are changing and that more young adults will have better treatment in the future.

There were so many times when Renee Turchi felt as if she were falling between the cracks. In 2005, after being diagnosed at age 33 with a rare, soft-tissue tumor in her lung, she found herself stuck between

SOURCE: Katherine Hobson, "Cancer's Orphan Generation," *U.S. News & World Report*, vol. 142, January 15, 2007, pp. 76–77. Copyright © 2007 U.S. News and World Report, L.P. All rights reserved. Reprinted with permission.

the worlds of adult and pediatric oncology. "Everybody else was running around playing with Legos," she says, or her chemotherapy roommates were all in their 60s or 70s or 80s. "I was so aware of being the youngest," says Turchi. "You tend to identify with your peer group. I couldn't find any adults with Ewing's sarcoma."

Turchi is hardly the public face of cancer, which is perceived to strike older adults and little kids, not those in the middle. And it's true that cancer strikes mostly those over age 65. But around 70,000 people between the ages of 15 and 39 in the United States are diagnosed with cancer each year, about eight times the number of youngsters who get the disease. Turchi's feelings of isolation are symbolic of what is happening in today's cancer wards to teens and young adults: While their survival rates used to be the envy of the cancer community—above 70 percent, on average—adolescents and young adults have gained very little from advances in treatment and detection over the past few decades. "Overall survival rates have plateaued, and there's been no improvement, while younger and older patients have improved," says Brandon Hayes-Lattin, director of the Adolescent and Young Adult Oncology Program at Oregon Health and Science University Cancer Institute in Portland. In some cancers, like certain lymphomas, survival rates have actually declined in this age group.

A Long-Term Plan of Attack

Cancer experts and healthcare providers are determined to reverse that trend. About 10 hospitals across the country have created special clinics or programs devoted to adolescents and young adults, the so-called AYAs. Two giants in the field, the National Cancer Institute (NCI) and the nonprofit Lance Armstrong Foundation (LAF), teamed up recently to map out a long-term plan of attack. And the LAF is reaching out to other research and advocacy organizations to coordinate efforts. The goal: to improve the survival prospects for what many are now calling the "orphan generation" of cancer.

A 10-year-old diagnosed with cancer in the late 1970s had about a 60 percent chance of surviving for five years. But a 10-year-old diagnosed in the '90s saw his odds upped to 75 percent. For a 65-year-old, the five-year survival rate leapt from about 45 percent to more than 65 percent. Then consider a 30-year-old: While she had a 70 percent chance of living for five years back then, her

Sixteen-year-old Jacky Sims bears a scar where a cancerous melanoma was removed from her skin. **(AP Images)**

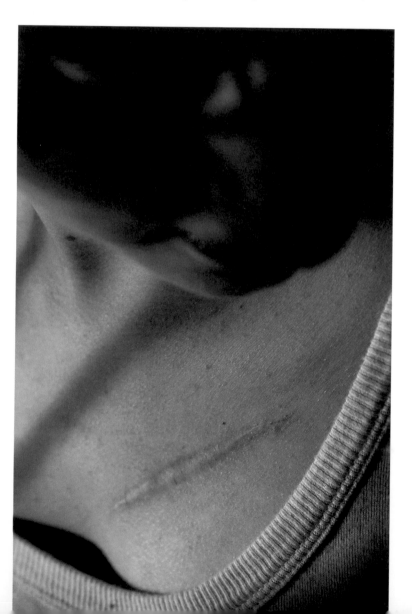

prognosis had actually slightly worsened by the late 1990s. Those trends continue into this decade, says Archie Bleyer, an oncologist and medical adviser at the cancer treatment center at St. Charles Medical Center in Bend, Ore., and a longtime researcher in the field.

Experts must first determine why survival rates have stalled. Researchers plan to study the characteristics of the particular cancers—such as lymphoma, melanoma, and genital cancers—that tend to be the most common in teens and young adults. They'll also delve into whether a cancer in young adults is different from the same type of cancer in adults and children and how that affects treatment. (Children, for example, can tolerate more chemo than older adults in part because their cells are furiously renewing as they grow.) Experts have already found some differences. Breast cancer, for example, tends to be more aggressive in younger women, says Karin Hahn, an oncologist at M.D. Anderson Cancer Center in Houston and head of its program for young breast cancer survivors. It's also less often fueled by estrogen, which means patients are less likely to benefit from the anti-estrogenic drugs like tamoxifen. The NCI/LAF group, which met in Austin in 2006, recommends that scientists first focus on certain sarcomas, non-Hodgkin's lymphoma, colorectal cancer, breast cancer, and cancers of the germ cells that become sperm or eggs. Those were picked because they're common enough to have a big impact, have shown little progress among this age group, and are often life threatening.

Clinical Trials Are Frequently for Children

One reason so little is known about cancer in young adults is that few of them participate in clinical trials, which provide both better care for participants and crucial information to help future patients. "Trial participation drops off markedly around age 19," says Doug Ulman, chief mission officer of the LAF and founder of the Ulman Cancer Fund

FAST FACT

Bone cancers appear most frequently in children and young adults, especially those who have experienced chemotherapy or radiation treatment.

for Young Adults. (Ulman, 29, has survived two bouts with melanoma and a cartilage tumor.) "If we can figure that out, we can start to make some strides," he says.

It could be as simple as time and transportation. While kids have Mom or Dad to organize their lives and drive them to and from treatment, young adults can't always get themselves to the treatment facility. Some trials have been closed to them, too, as most have age cutoffs. Researchers say that those limits should be reconsidered and that there's a need for more trials specific to this age group. And to attract more patients, trials should work around impediments such as school, job schedules, and child care.

Access to Care Can Be a Barrier

Also keeping a lid on survival rates is access to care, says Karen Albritton, who is developing the AYA program at Dana-Farber Cancer Institute in Boston. As AYAs are more apt to have entry-level jobs with no benefits or be between jobs, they're more likely to be uninsured and thus probably don't see a doctor regularly. And because neither they nor their doctors suspect cancer at first, often their disease isn't caught in its earliest, most treatable stages.

Take lung cancer survivor Dan Waeger, who was working on his M.B.A., coaching college golf, and training for a marathon when he was diagnosed in 2005, just before his 23rd birthday. "I didn't know a single person with cancer," he says, and he never imagined that his months of coughing could portend such a diagnosis. Waeger is now undergoing chemotherapy and just months after his diagnosis founded the National Collegiate Cancer Foundation, which provides need-based financial aid for kids with cancer who want to continue with college.

New Programs for Young Adults

The new programs at hospitals and cancer centers aim to serve as research hubs for trials specifically for teens and young adults. The programs have dedicated staff and special support groups and outside activities like retreats geared to these in-betweeners. Perhaps most important, the distinct life stage of this age group can be addressed. "We have to tell them, 'We may make you infertile, we will make you bald, we will make you gain and lose weight,'" says Megan Burke, medical director of the new AYA program at the Cleveland Clinic. Those worries loom large among young adults, and some have practical

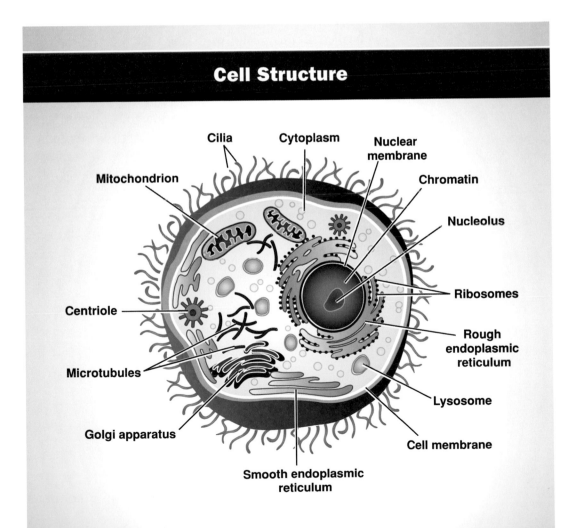

Cell Structure

Cilia
Cytoplasm
Nuclear membrane
Mitochondrion
Chromatin
Nucleolus
Ribosomes
Centriole
Rough endoplasmic reticulum
Microtubules
Lysosome
Golgi apparatus
Cell membrane
Smooth endoplasmic reticulum

solutions, like bringing in fertility experts or weighing the long-term effects of chemotherapy on the heart.

The centers are also magnets for young people, who can act as ad hoc support groups. Heidi Adams, 39, a sarcoma survivor who now runs Planet Cancer (www.planetcancer.org) for young adults affected by cancer, recalls a support group she once attended where she felt surrounded by her grandparents. "I thought, 'You don't understand that I'm not dating, that I can't keep up with my friends, that I feel like my life is on hold, that I'm facing mortality for the first time,'" she says. But among peers, young adults can connect and talk about their concerns, such as sex during treatment, how to deal with overprotective parents, and, for some, facing death.

Thanks to the newfound scrutiny, that last, most frightening scenario should confront fewer young people, says Bleyer, who has spent years trying to call attention to the discrepancy. "The momentum can't be denied, and I can sit back and enjoy that." So will the teens and young adults whose lives stand to be saved.

Recent Advancement in Breast Cancer Research

Reuters Limited

The author of the following article presents researchers' discovery of the first common breast cancer susceptibility gene. According to researchers, the mutations in the gene, which is called FGFR2, raise the risk of breast cancer by 20 to 60 percent. While it is too soon to screen women for these gene variants, the discovery is a promising advancement in research for this disease which kills five-hundred thousand people a year globally.

Agenetic mutation that raises the risk of breast cancer is found in up to 60 percent of U.S. women, making it the first truly common breast cancer susceptibility gene, researchers reported in May 2007.

Breast Cancer Genetics

Reports from several teams around the world identified changes in four other genes that raise the risk of breast

SOURCE: Reuters Limited, "Common Breast Cancer Genes Found," MSNBC.com, May 27, 2007. Copyright © 2007 Reuters Limited. Reproduced by permission.

cancer significantly. Several are found in many men and women.

More than 60 percent of the women in the United States probably carry at least one of the mutations in one of the genes, called FGFR2, the researchers said.

"This is a truly landmark breakthrough for breast cancer research, because these genes are the first confirmed common genetic risk factors for breast cancer," said Jianjun Liu of the Genome Institute of Singapore, who took part in one of the studies.

The researchers, reporting in the journals *Nature* and *Nature Genetics*, said the discoveries are the most impor-

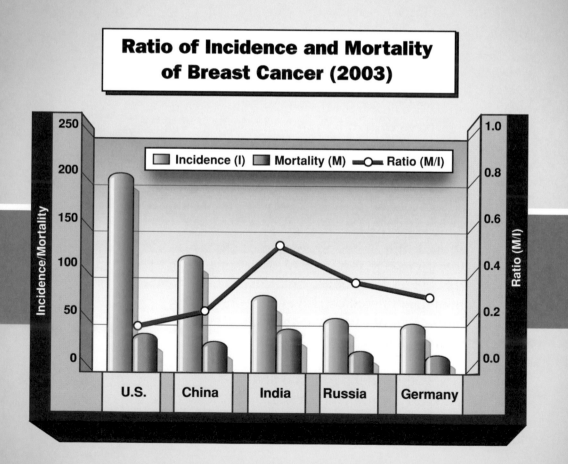

Source: Abstract from Biotechnology Decision Support Database, Frost and Sullivan.

tant genes associated with breast cancer since BRCA1 and BRCA2 were identified.

Further Results

Women with faulty copies of BRCA1 or BRCA2 have a 50 percent to 85 percent chance of getting breast cancer in their lifetimes. But they are rare genes, and only account for 5 percent to possibly 10 percent of breast cancer cases.

Researchers have been testing women for other genes associated with breast cancer, to find its causes, to understand how and why it develops, and to make more effective treatments.

Better techniques to analyze DNA, and the publication of the human genome, the map of all DNA in the body, have made this a much faster and easier process. David Hunter of Harvard University and a team at the U.S. National Cancer Institute looked at more than 2,200 women of European ancestry.

> ## FAST FACT
>
> Women who have two copies of the high risk variants of the gene FGFR2 have a 20 to 60 percent greater chance of getting breast cancer compared with women who have none.

Common Gene, Big Risk

They found four common mutations in FGFR2 associated with the breast cancer in women after menopause who do not have known relatives with breast cancer.

The mutations raise the risk of breast cancer risk by 20 percent if they carry one copy of the gene and by 60 percent if they carry two copies. And close to 60 percent of the women they studied carried at least one copy.

The findings do not yet have any real relevance for women, Hunter stressed.

Too Soon for Genetic Screening?

"It is premature to recommend screening women for these gene variants, at least until the scientific community has further combed through the genome-wide findings and

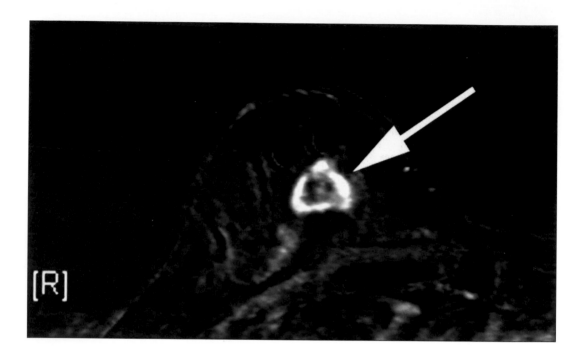

A magnetic resonance imaging (MRI) scan of this fifty-five-year-old woman's breast has detected a cancerous tumor, as indicated by the arrow. (AP Images)

found all the variants that are associated with increased risk," Hunter said in a statement.

Douglas Easton of Britain's University of Cambridge led a team of researchers around the world to look at tiny changes in the DNA code called single nucleotide polymorphisms or SNPs—pronounced "snips"—in the DNA of 21,860 people with breast cancer and 22,578 people without it.

They found mutations in four genes that were more common in the people with breast cancer—FGFR2, TNRC9, MAP3K1 and LSP1.

A Logical Candidate

FGFR2 may be a logical candidate for a breast cancer gene—it is a receptor, a kind of molecular doorway, for a compound called tyrosine kinase which is involved in several cancers.

In a third study, a team at deCODE genetics, the University of Nijmegen in the Netherlands and elsewhere studied 22,000 people to find two other gene mutations associated with breast cancer. One is also near TNRC9.

"DeCODE estimates that these two variants are contributing factors in one quarter of breast cancer cases in women of European origin," the company wrote in a statement.

Breast cancer kills 500,000 people a year globally according to the World Health Organization, and 1.2 million men and women are diagnosed with it every year.

Gene Therapy May Hold the Key to a Cancer Cure

Ingrid Wickelgren

The following article by Ingrid Wickelgren recounts the treatment of Mark Origer, a patient with deadly melanoma. Doctors at the National Cancer Institute were experimenting with a new treatment that they tested on Origer and others. Wickelgren describes how the doctors removed some of the white blood cells and altered them genetically to make them more effective in fighting the cancer. Wickelgren reports that the treatment worked on Origer and another patient in the test. While the tests were small and need further research, Wickelgren concludes that the therapy offers promise for the future.

Two years ago, doctors told Mark Origer that he had about three months to live. Origer, 51, had a deadly form of skin cancer, a disease in which abnormal cells grow without limit. The disease started as a

SOURCE: Ingrid Wickelgren, "An Answer to Cancer? A New Therapy Treats Cancer by Altering Patient's DNA," *Current Science*, vol. 92, January 19, 2007, pp. 6–11. Copyright © 2007 Weekly Reader Corporation. Reproduced by permission.

black mole on Origer's back and then metastasized (spread) to other parts of his body.

Doctors tried surgically removing the cancerous tumors, or clumps of cells, but failed to get all of them. The cancer returned. Origer's doctors then gave him two drugs to urge the body's disease-fighting immune system to kill the cancer. But the cancer kept coming back.

In December 2004, Origer was very sick and he seemed out of options. His daughter Katie was getting married in six months, but nobody expected him to live that long. "He was anxious to do almost anything that would get him to his daughter's wedding," says one of his doctors, Steven Rosenberg, a cancer specialist at the National Cancer Institute in Bethesda, Md.

Fortunately, Rosenberg was about to test a brand-new treatment for melanoma, the deadliest form of skin cancer and the form that Origer had. Because no standard treatment had worked for Origer, he was an excellent candidate for Rosenberg's experimental therapy.

Genetically Altered White Cells Fight Tumors

Rosenberg had developed a cancer treatment that recruits a patient's own white blood cells, the soldiers of the immune system. The treatment involves removing white blood cells from the patient's body and selecting the ones that are armed to fight tumors. The armed cells carry molecules, called receptor proteins on their surfaces that match distinctive molecules on the cancer cells. The matching receptor proteins enable the white blood cells to home in on a tumor and eradicate it.

Rosenberg made the tumor-fighting cells grow like mad in his laboratory: he then injected them back into the patient. Using the patient's own cells prevented the body's immune system from rejecting, or killing, the cells. The immune system rejects cells and tissues that are foreign—not from that patient.

Rosenberg tried the cell therapy on 35 people with melanoma, and half of them improved; their tumors shrank. Three patients even went into remission, a state in which the disease is temporarily or permanently gone. But finding the best cancer-killing white blood cells is difficult, and not all patients have many of them. So Rosenberg and his research team added a twist to the therapy. They devised a way to transform ordinary white blood cells into aggressive tumor killers.

How did they do that? They injected genes for the tumor-killing receptor proteins into the white blood cells. Genes are pieces of DNA that instruct a cell to make certain protein molecules. Researchers often use viruses to carry the new genes into cells. The tactic of treating disease by altering cells' genes is called gene therapy.

By late 2004, the scientists were ready to try the gene therapy on Origer. Rosenberg's study included 16 other patients whose melanoma was likely to kill them. In all the patients, the standard treatments had failed.

Gene Therapy Offers Hope

In the first three patients who received the new gene therapy, the transformed cells did not last long inside the body. The therapy failed. But when the scientists drew blood from Origer, they put the transformed blood cells back into his body sooner, when the cells were still rapidly multiplying. As a result, many of the cancer-fighting cells survived in his body for weeks. The researchers used the improved technique on the rest of the patients in the study as well.

Most of the 17 patients did not get better. But two of them, Origer and one other man, did. A small tumor in Origer's armpit disappeared completely, and a big tumor in his liver shrank by almost 90 percent; doctors removed

FAST FACT

Genetic testing can determine the risk of getting cancer, but these tests cannot predict with absolute certainty.

Mark Origer and his daughter Katie on her wedding day in 2005. (AP Images)

the rest of it surgically. In the other man, a lung tumor shrank to nothing.

Often, therapies have side effects unintended, harmful effects on the body that are caused by a drug or a treatment. But Rosenberg's new therapy did not appear to produce any side effects.

Skeptics have pointed out that Rosenberg's study was small and that it helped only a small fraction of the people enrolled. Still, the success stories are encouraging;

The Number of Gene Therapy Trials Worldwide Initiated Between 1993–2003

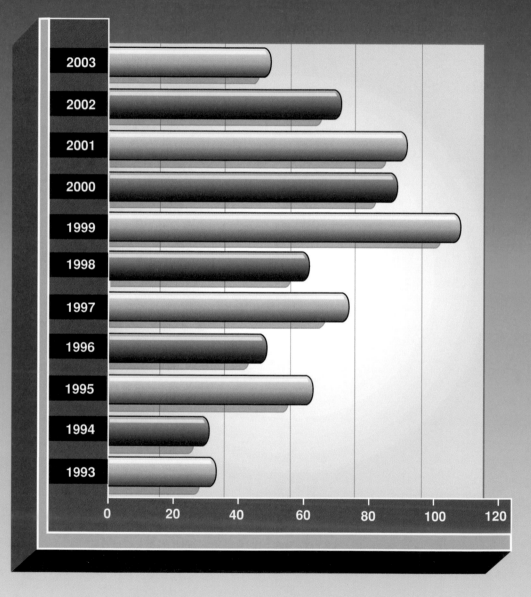

Source: *The Journal of Gene Medicine*, 2004, John Wiley and Sons Ltd., Billam AG.

recovery in patients with advanced forms of melanoma is extremely rare. Standard therapy works for only 15 percent of patients whose melanomas have spread, Rosenberg says, so many patients like Origer need another option. Melanoma kills about 8,000 Americans each year.

Therapy May Be Effective on Other Cancers

Rosenberg says his therapy might be used to treat other types of cancer. In such cases, doctors would insert genes into white blood cells that make receptor proteins that match specific molecules on, say, breast, lung, or other tumors. "This represents a new approach for treating cancer," Rosenberg told *Current Science*. "We can introduce genes that can affect almost any property of a cell."

Six months after Origer signed up for the experiment, he walked Katie down the aisle at her wedding. He is still alive today [January 2007].

A New Drug Attacks Only Cancer Cells

Andy Coghlan

Andy Coghlan has been writing for *New Scientist* for almost twenty years. In this article he describes the research done by a team from the University of Alberta, who have discovered a new use for an old drug. The team examined the way in which cancerous cells generate energy, Coghlan writes. A drug called dichloroacetate (DCA), which has been used for other disorders, can change the energy source of a cancerous cell and cause it to self-destruct. It has proven to be relatively safe, Coghlan says, and since it is out of patent it would be affordable. The next step is to conduct clinical trials.

It sounds almost too good to be true: a cheap and simple drug that kills almost all cancers by switching off their "immortality". The drug, dichloroacetate (DCA), has already been used for years to treat rare metabolic disorders and so is known to be relatively safe. It also has no patent, meaning it could be manufactured

SOURCE: Andy Coghlan, "Cheap, Safe Drug Kills Most Cancers," *New Scientist*, vol. 193, January 20, 2007, p. 13. Copyright © 2007 Reed Elsevier Business Publishing, Ltd. Reproduced by permission.

for a fraction of the cost of newly developed drugs.

Evangelos Michelakis of the University of Alberta in Edmonton, Canada, and his colleagues tested DCA on human cells cultured outside the body and found that it killed lung, breast and brain cancer cells, but not healthy cells. Tumours in rats deliberately infected with human cancer also shrank drastically when they were fed DCA-laced water for several weeks.

DCA attacks a unique feature of cancer cells: the fact that they make their energy throughout the main body of the cell, rather than in distinct organelles called mitochondria. This process, called glycolysis, is inefficient and uses up vast amounts of sugar. Until now it had been assumed that cancer cells used glycolysis because their mitochondria were irreparably damaged. However, Michelakis's experiments prove this is not the case, because DCA reawakened the mitochondria in cancer cells. The cells then withered and died.

Michelakis suggests that the switch to glycolysis as an energy source occurs when cells in the middle of an abnormal but benign lump don't get enough oxygen for their mitochondria to work properly. In order to survive, they switch off their mitochondria and start producing energy through glycolysis.

Drug Causes Cancer Cells to Self-Destruct

Crucially, though, mitochondria do another job in cells: they activate apoptosis, the process by which abnormal cells self-destruct. When cells switch mitochondria off, they become "immortal", outliving other cells in the tumour and so becoming dominant. Once reawakened by DCA, mitochondria reactivate apoptosis and order the abnormal cells to die.

> **FAST FACT**
>
> The number of people dying from cancer increases each year because the population is increasing. The rate of death from cancer is actually decreasing.

"The results are intriguing because they point to a critical role that mitochondria play: they impart a unique trait to cancer cells that can be exploited for cancer therapy," says Dario Altieri, director of the University of Massachusetts Cancer Center in Worcester.

The phenomenon might also explain how secondary cancers form. Glycolysis generates lactic acid, which can break down the collagen matrix holding cells together. This means abnormal cells can be released and float to other parts of the body, where they seed new tumours. DCA can cause pain, numbness and gait disturbances in some patients, but this may be a price worth paying if it

What Makes Cancer Cells Different — and How to Kill Them

Normal cells (green) in the middle of a benign growth are starved of oxygen but can survive by switching to glycolysis, a different way of making energy. In the process the mitochondria, which contain the cells' self-destruct mechanism, switch it off. This makes the cells "immortal" and cancerous (red), so they carry on replicating and the tumor grows.

Glycolysis also generates lactic acid, which lets the cancer cells eat through tissue, escape, and form secondary cancers elsewhere in the body.

A drug called dichloroacetate switches the mitochondria in the cancer cells back on (green) so they halt glycolysis and start making energy in mitochondria again. The self-destruct mechanism is then activated, and the cells wither and die (brown).

Source: Newscientist.com.

turns out to be effective against all cancers. The next step is to run clinical trials of DCA in people with cancer. These may have to be funded by charities, universities and governments: pharmaceutical companies are unlikely to pay because they can't make money on unpatented medicines. The pay-off is that if DCA does work, it will be easy to manufacture and dirt cheap.

Paul Clarke, a cancer cell biologist at the University of Dundee in the UK, says the findings challenge the current assumption that mutations, not metabolism, spark off cancers. "The question is: which comes first?" he says.

Prostate Cancer: The Most Commonly Diagnosed Cancer in Men

Tedd Mitchell

In the following article, Tedd Mitchell explains that prostate cancer can occur in younger men as well as older men. He discusses the importance of preventative measures and a healthy lifestyle to reduce the risk or severity of prostate cancer. Mitchell asserts that new developments in the treatment of prostate cancer provide hope for those with this disease.

Tedd Mitchell is a doctor who writes a weekly column for *USA Today*.

Joe was 55 and feeling good when he visited his urologist in 1997. Because of increasing levels of PSA (prostate specific antigen) in his blood, a screening test for prostate cancer, a biopsy was done. It revealed cancer. Surgery and radiation followed. Joe still sees the urologist and a radiation specialist every six months.

Joe's story is like many men's. His father had prostate cancer, but not until his 70s. Joe never had prostate prob-

SOURCE: Tedd Mitchell, "Overcoming Prostate Cancer," *USA Weekend*, June 2, 2002. Copyright © 2002 USA Today. Reproduced by permission.

lems, so being diagnosed with the cancer was shocking. But Joe, now 60, is a survivor with an upbeat attitude. He and [Joe's wife] Nancy, 58, are big believers in complementary medicine (in fact, Joe swears that grapefruit fiber, soy and IP6 supplements have kept his PSA down), and they see an acupuncturist several times a year for stress, back pain and sinus relief.

Prostate Cancer: Not Just for "Old" People

What can we learn from Joe's situation? For starters, prostate cancer is not just for "old" people. Most cases do occur after age 65, but improved screening techniques make it possible to find cancers in much younger men.

For years, the gold standard of diagnosis was the digital rectal examination (the "finger wave" exam). It's still integral, but the PSA blood test is an increasingly standard part of the health screen for men older than 50. It's widely available and useful in detecting cancer at much earlier stages, when therapy can improve quantity and quality of life. And today's treatments cause fewer side effects.

Testing and Treatments

The American Cancer Society and the American Urological Association recommend annual PSA tests, along with the digital rectal examination, for men over 50 and for high-risk men over 40. Men at particular risk include blacks (who have twice the risk of whites) and those with a family history of prostate cancer. Although the PSA is a good test, it's not the be-all and end-all. PSA levels can be elevated by other conditions. The "free PSA" specialized test can help distinguish between benign and cancerous elevations. Other maneuvers, such as following how rapidly the PSA changes, also can

FAST FACT

About one man in six will be diagnosed with prostate cancer during his lifetime, but only one man in 34 will die of this disease.

Survival Rate After Prostate Cancer Diagnosis

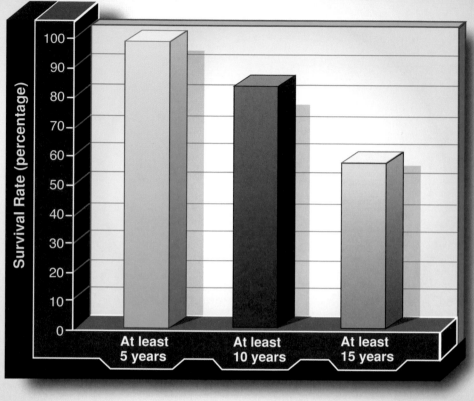

Source: The American Cancer Society.

be informative. That was true in Joe's case. His doctors had been watching a rising PSA level, so they ordered further testing.

If prostate cancer has been diagnosed, the next step is to determine the extent of the disease. A series of tests measure the size of the tumor in the prostate and find whether it has spread to other parts of the body. That helps to direct therapy.

Treatments include surgery, radiation, cryotherapy (freezing tumor cells), chemotherapy/hormonal therapy and newer options, such as brachytherapy and proton therapy.

All Are a "Good News/Bad News" Proposition.

The good news: Therapies are more effective.

The bad news: complications. Side effects have improved significantly, but patients still can have problems with urinary incontinence, impotence, pain and diarrhea (to name a few), depending on the type and extent of their therapy. Accordingly, elderly men who have other health problems sometimes opt to simply monitor this

Urologist Craig Zippe holds a tube of Viadur. It is designed to be implanted under the skin of a patient, where it can dispense a steady dose of drugs to fight prostate cancer over the course of a year. (**AP Images**)

slow-growing cancer. For example, if an older man has extensive heart disease that soon will end his life, it may not be worth putting him through aggressive therapies to treat a small tumor. The bottom line is that treatment of prostate cancer is effective and varied, and it requires informed discussions with a prostate cancer specialist.

New Advancements

Exciting things are on the horizon. New drugs are being evaluated that may kill prostate cancer cells by destroying their blood supply. Additionally, vaccinations are being evaluated to stimulate the immune system to rid itself of potential problem cells.

Our generation may not enjoy the full benefit of this research, but our children very likely will deal with prostate cancer in a completely different way.

Meanwhile, a man's lifestyle can help prevent prostate cancer. High-fat diets have been associated with an increased risk of prostate cancer, while soy protein and tomatoes may reduce the risk. Vitamin E supplements may reduce the risk, too, according to a study conducted at the National Cancer Institute.

CHAPTER 2

Controversies in Cancer Treatment

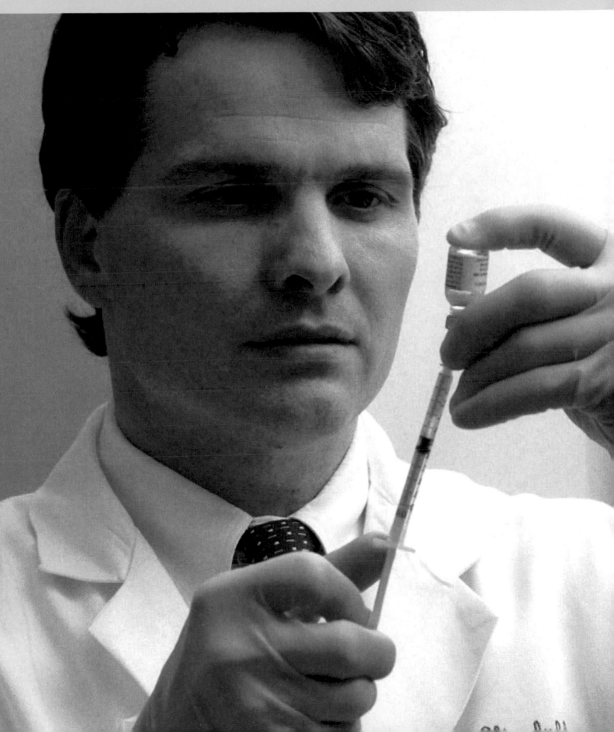

Secondhand Smoke Causes Cancer

Richard H. Carmona

Vice Admiral Richard H. Carmona is a former Surgeon General of the United States. In the following article, Carmona notes that the dangers of secondhand smoke have been verified for over twenty years. Secondhand smoke is the cause of lung cancer, heart disease, and other health problems. There is no safe level, Carmona asserts. He remains concerned that millions of Americans are exposed to the hazards of secondhand smoke. Establishing smoke-free environments is the only way to minimize the dangers posed by smoke.

Photo on previous page. Dr. Craig Singluff works in his lab at the University of Virginia as he tries to develop a vaccine against melanoma. **(AP Images)**

Twenty years ago the 1986 Surgeon General's Report on *The Health Consequences of Involuntary Smoking* concluded that secondhand smoke exposure was a cause of disease in nonsmokers. That Report, which was one of the first major reports to investigate this topic, concluded that secondhand smoke caused lung cancer among nonsmoking adults and several res-

SOURCE: Richard H. Carmona, MD, MPH, FACS, United States Surgeon General, remarks at a press conference, June 27, 2006.

piratory problems among children. Since that Report was published, hundreds of peer-reviewed studies and several additional major reports on the health effects of secondhand smoke have been published, and the evidence on these health effects has become even stronger.

The Surgeon General's Report that we are releasing today, *The Health Consequences of Involuntary Exposure to Tobacco Smoke*, documents beyond any doubt that secondhand smoke harms people's health. In the course of the past 20 years, the scientific community has reached consensus on this point.

I would like to draw your attention to several new conclusions that I have reached due to overwhelming scientific evidence.

- Secondhand smoke exposure causes heart disease and lung cancer in adults and sudden infant death syndrome and respiratory problems in children.
- There is NO risk-free level of secondhand smoke exposure, with even brief exposure adversely affecting the cardiovascular and respiratory system.
- Only smoke-free environments effectively protect nonsmokers from secondhand smoke exposure in indoor spaces.
- Finally, the Report concludes that, while great strides have been made in recent years in reducing nonsmoking Americans' secondhand smoke exposure, millions of Americans continue to be exposed to secondhand smoke in their homes and workplaces.

Secondhand Smoke Is Harmful to All People

Allow me to expand on the first major conclusion. Secondhand smoke is a health hazard for all people: it is harmful to both children and adults, and to both women and men. It is harmful to nonsmokers whether they are exposed in their homes, their vehicles, their workplaces,

Secondhand Smoke Is Toxic

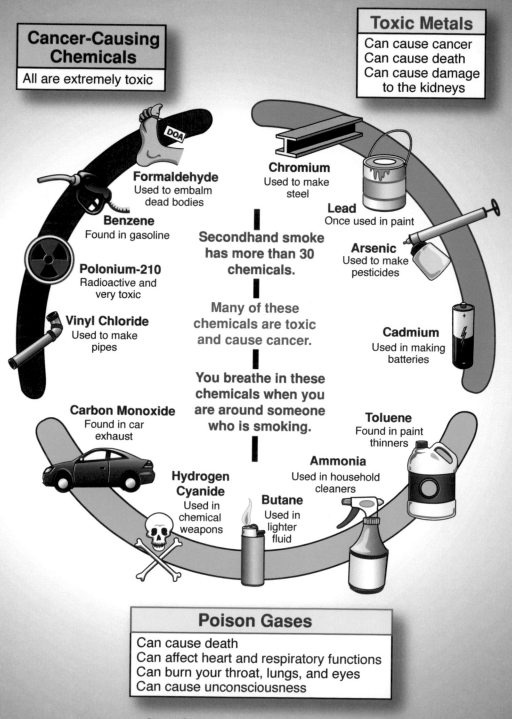

Cancer-Causing Chemicals

All are extremely toxic

Toxic Metals

Can cause cancer
Can cause death
Can cause damage to the kidneys

Formaldehyde
Used to embalm dead bodies

Benzene
Found in gasoline

Polonium-210
Radioactive and very toxic

Vinyl Chloride
Used to make pipes

Chromium
Used to make steel

Lead
Once used in paint

Arsenic
Used to make pesticides

Cadmium
Used in making batteries

Secondhand smoke has more than 30 chemicals.

Many of these chemicals are toxic and cause cancer.

You breathe in these chemicals when you are around someone who is smoking.

Carbon Monoxide
Found in car exhaust

Hydrogen Cyanide
Used in chemical weapons

Butane
Used in lighter fluid

Ammonia
Used in household cleaners

Toluene
Found in paint thinners

Poison Gases

Can cause death
Can affect heart and respiratory functions
Can burn your throat, lungs, and eyes
Can cause unconsciousness

Source: Centers for Disease Control and Prevention.

or in enclosed public places. We have found that certain populations are especially susceptible to the health effects of secondhand smoke, including infants and children, pregnant women, older persons, and persons with pre-existing respiratory conditions and heart disease. It is not surprising that secondhand smoke is so harmful. Nonsmokers who are exposed to secondhand smoke inhale the same toxins and cancer-causing substances as smokers. Secondhand smoke has been found to contain more than 50 carcinogens and at least 250 chemicals that are known to be toxic or carcinogenic. This helps explain why nonsmokers who are exposed to secondhand smoke develop some of the same diseases that smokers do.

Health Effects of Exposure to Secondhand Smoke in Adults

Let's look first at the health effects that secondhand smoke causes in adults.

Lung Cancer

The Report confirms that secondhand smoke is a known human carcinogen that causes lung cancer in nonsmoking adults. Nonsmokers who are exposed to secondhand smoke, at home or at work, increase their risk of developing lung cancer by 20 percent to 30 percent. Secondhand smoke causes approximately 3,000 lung cancer deaths among U.S. nonsmokers each year.

Heart Disease

The Report released today also concludes that secondhand smoke causes heart disease. Nonsmoking adults who are exposed to secondhand smoke at home or at work increase their risk of developing heart disease by 25 to 30 percent. The evidence indicates that even brief secondhand smoke exposures can have immediate adverse effects on the cardiovascular system. This is especially true for persons who already have heart disease, or who are at special risk of heart disease. Secondhand smoke causes tens of thousands of heart disease deaths each year among U.S. nonsmokers. . . .

There Is No Risk-Free Level of Exposure to Secondhand Smoke

We know that secondhand smoke harms people's health, but many people assume that exposure to secondhand smoke in small doses does not do any significant damage to one's health. However, science has proven that there is NO risk-free level of exposure to secondhand smoke. Let me say that again: there is no safe level of exposure to second-hand smoke. Breathing secondhand smoke for even a short time can damage cells and set the cancer process in motion. Brief exposure can have immediate harmful effects on blood and blood vessels, potentially increasing the risk of a heart attack. Secondhand smoke exposure can quickly irritate the lungs, or trigger an asthma attack. For some people, these rapid effects can be life-threatening. People who already have heart disease or respiratory conditions are at especially high risk.

FAST FACT

Secondhand smoke may be responsible for 3,400 fatal cases of lung cancer among nonsmokers each year.

Establishing Smoke-Free Environments Is the Only Proven Way to Prevent Exposure

The good news is that, unlike some public health hazards, secondhand smoke exposure is preventable. A proven method exists for protecting nonsmokers from the health risks associated with secondhand smoke exposure: avoiding places where secondhand smoke is present. An important new conclusion of this Report is that smoke-free environments are the ONLY approach that effectively protects nonsmokers from the dangers of secondhand smoke. The 1986 Surgeon General's Report concluded that the simple separation of smokers and nonsmokers within the same air space may reduce, but does not eliminate, secondhand smoke exposure among nonsmokers. The current Report expands on that finding by concluding that even sophisticated ventilation approaches cannot completely remove secondhand smoke from an indoor space. Because there is no risk-free level of secondhand smoke exposure, anything less cannot ensure that nonsmokers are fully protected from the dangers of exposure to secondhand smoke.

Arkansans for Drug-Free Youth rally on the steps of the Arkansas Capitol in 2006 in support of a law that would ban smoking in the workplace. Behind them are 700 pairs of shoes, symbolizing deaths caused each year by secondhand smoke. (**AP Images**)

Many Americans Remain at Risk

The good news is that we are making progress. Secondhand smoke exposure among U.S. nonsmokers has declined since the publication of the 1986 Surgeon General's Report. Levels of cotinine, the biomarker of secondhand smoke exposure, fell by 70 percent from 1988–91 to 2001–02. The proportion of nonsmokers with detectable cotinine levels has been halved from 88 percent to 43 percent.

However, while we have made great strides over the years to reduce smoking in America, the success story is not complete. More than 126 million nonsmoking Americans, including both children and adults, are still exposed to secondhand smoke in their homes and workplaces. Given the extensive evidence on the serious health risks posed by secondhand smoke exposure that is reviewed in the Report we are releasing today, the involuntary nature of this exposure, and the availability of a proven method for eliminating these risks, we cannot be satisfied until all Americans are aware of the health hazards caused by secondhand smoke on their families and loved ones.

Secondhand Smoke May Not Cause Cancer

James E. Enstrom and Geoffrey C. Kabat

James E. Enstrom is a professor at UCLA School of Public Health and Jonsson Comprehensive Cancer Center. Geoffrey C. Kabat is with the Division of Epidemiology of the American Health Foundation. This technical study reports on a long-term study of smokers and their nonsmoking spouses. The authors state that previous studies have been questionable because environmental tobacco smoke is difficult to measure accurately. The researchers tracked over 118,000 participants in the study, including 35,000 nonsmokers whose spouses were smokers, over a thirty-year period. They conclude that only a weak relationship—if that—exists between heart disease and lung cancer and secondhand smoke.

Several major reviews have determined that exposure to environmental tobacco smoke increases the relative risk of coronary heart disease, based primarily

SOURCE: James E. Enstrom and Geoffrey C. Kabat, "Environmental Tobacco Smoke and Tobacco Related Mortality in a Prospective Study of Californians, 1960–98," *British Medical Journal*, vol. 326, May 17, 2003, pp. 1057–1062. Copyright © 2003 British Medical Association. Reproduced by permission.

on comparing never smokers married to smokers with never smokers married to never smokers. The American Heart Association, the California Environmental Protection Agency, and the US surgeon general have concluded that the increase in coronary heart disease risk due to environmental tobacco smoke is 30% (relative risk 1.30). Meta-analyses of epidemiological studies have reported summary relative risks of about 1.30 for coronary heart disease and about 1.25 for lung cancer. The US Environmental Protection Agency has classified environmental tobacco smoke as a known human carcinogen. Chronic obstructive pulmonary disease, primarily asthma, bronchitis, and emphysema, has been associated with exposure to environmental tobacco smoke, but the evidence for increased mortality is sparse.

Although these reviews come to similar conclusions, the association between environmental tobacco smoke

Jeff Allen and others smoke at the Pegasus Restaurant in Tacoma, Washington, as part of a "smoke-in" protest against an indoor smoking ban. (AP Images)

and tobacco related diseases is still controversial owing to several limitations in the epidemiological studies. Exposure to environmental tobacco smoke is difficult to measure quantitatively and therefore has been approximated by self reported estimates, primarily smoking history in spouses. Confounding by active cigarette smoking is so strong that the association with environmental tobacco smoke can only be evaluated among never smokers. The relation between tobacco related diseases and environmental tobacco smoke may be influenced by misclassification of some smokers as never smokers, misclassification of exposure status to environmental tobacco smoke, and several potential confounders. It is also unclear how the reported increased risk of coronary heart disease due to environmental tobacco smoke could be so close to the increased risk due to active smoking, since environmental tobacco smoke is much more dilute than actively inhaled smoke.

> **FAST FACT**
>
> The World Health Organization estimates that 40 percent of all cancers can be prevented by eating right, exercising, and not smoking.

Most epidemiological studies have found that environmental tobacco smoke has a positive but not statistically significant relation to coronary heart disease and lung cancer. Meta-analyses have combined these inconclusive results to produce statistically significant summary relative risks. However, there are problems inherent in using meta-analysis to establish a causal relation. The epidemiological data are subject to the limitations described above. They have not been collected in a standardized way, and some relative risks have been inappropriately combined. Because it is more likely that positive associations get published, unpublished negative results could reduce the summary relative risks. Also, the meta-analysis on coronary heart disease omitted the published negative results from the large American Cancer Society cancer prevention study. (GPSI). We have extended the follow up for the California participants in this cohort, analysed the relation between environmental tobacco smoke and tobacco related diseases, and addressed concerns about this study.

Methods

CPS-I is a prospective cohort study begun by the American Cancer Society in October 1959. Long term follow up was undertaken at the University of California at Los Angeles on all 118,094 participants from California (see bmj.com for details). In mid-1999 we sent out a two page questionnaire on smoking and lifestyle. The follow up period was from time of entry to the study (1 January to 31 March 1960) until death, withdrawal (date last known alive), or end of follow up (31 December 1998). The participants were aged 30–96 years at enrolment.

The underlying cause of each death was assigned according to the international classification of diseases. (seventh, eighth, or ninth revision). For the analysis of environmental tobacco smoke we selected the 35,561 participants who had never smoked as of 1959 and who had a spouse in the study with known smoking habits.

Statistical Analysis

The independent variable used for analysis was exposure to environmental tobacco smoke based on smoking status of the spouse in 1959, 1965, and 1972. Never smokers married to current or former smokers were compared with never smokers married to never smokers. The never smokers were defined as those who had never smoked any form of tobacco by the time of assessment. Never smokers married to a current smoker were subdivided into categories according to the smoking status of their spouse: 1–9, 10–19, 20, 21–39, ⩾40 cigarettes consumed per day for men and women, along with pipe or cigar usage for women. Former smokers were considered as an additional category.

We calculated the age adjusted relative risk of death and 95% confidence interval as a function of smoking status of the spouse by using Cox proportional hazards regression. A fully adjusted relative risk was calculated by using a model that included age and seven potential confounders at baseline: race (white, non-white), education level (<12, 12, >12 years), exercise (none or slight, moderate, heavy), body mass index (<20, 20-22.99, 23-25.99, 26-29.99, ⩾30), urbanisation (five population sizes), fruit or fruit juice intake (0-2, 3-4, 5-7 days a week), and health status (good, fair, poor, sick).

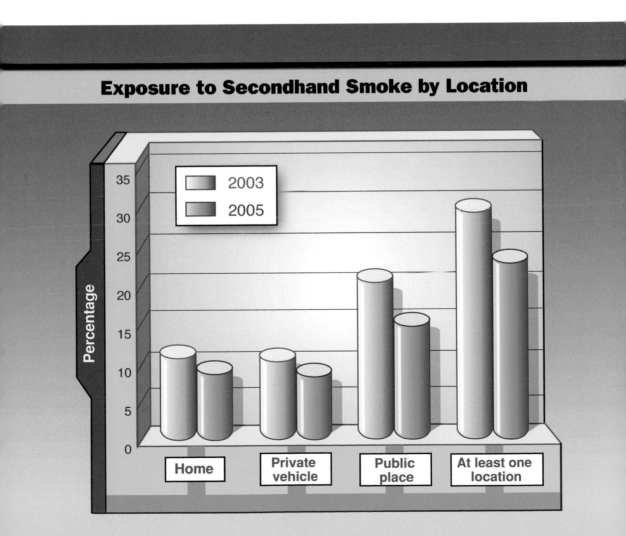

Exposure to Secondhand Smoke by Location

Results

The personal and lifestyle characteristics and follow up status for 1959 never smokers were relatively independent of their spouse's smoking status (see bmj.com). Also, the baseline characteristics of the 1999 respondents in 1959 were similar to those for all participants in 1959, except for a younger age at enrolment. Although heavily censored by age, the 1999 respondents seemed reasonably representative of survivors. Race, education, exercise, height, weight, and fruit intake had also remained largely unchanged among the 1999 respondents since 1959. The proportion of participants who had withdrawn as of 1972, were lost as of 1999, or had an unknown cause of death was not related to the smoking status of spouses. However, widowhood (widowed as of 1999) increased substantially with increased smoking in the spouse.

Effects of Exposure

Environmental Tobacco Smoke

Exposure to environmental tobacco smoke was not significantly associated with the death rate for coronary heart disease, lung cancer, or chronic obstructive pulmonary disease in men or women. The relative risks were slightly reduced after adjustment for seven confounders. The relative risks were consistent with 1.0 for virtually every level of exposure to environmental tobacco smoke, current or former. Only the relative risks for chronic obstructive pulmonary disease suggested an association. An environmental tobacco smoke index based on seven or eight levels of smoking in a spouse gave a relative risk of about 1.0 for each level of change and no suggestion of a dose-response trend.

Active Cigarette Smoking

As expected, there was a strong, positive dose-response relation between active cigarette smoking and deaths from coronary heart disease, lung cancer, and chronic obstructive pulmonary disease during 1960–98 (see bmj.com). These relative risks were consistent with those for the full CPS I cohort until 1972. As it is generally considered that exposure to environmental tobacco smoke is roughly equivalent to smoking one cigarette per day, we extrapolated the relative risk due to exposure to environmental tobacco smoke from the relative risks for smoking 1–9 cigarettes per day. These extrapolated relative risks were about 1.03 for coronary heart disease and about 1.20 for lung cancer and chronic obstructive pulmonary disease. Based on these findings, exposure to environmental tobacco smoke could not plausibly cause a 30% increase in risk of coronary heart disease in this cohort, although a 20% increase in risk of lung cancer and chronic obstructive pulmonary disease could not be ruled out.

Discussion

Our findings are based on the California cohort from the large American Cancer Society cancer prevention study (CPS) I), followed during 1960–98. Although participants in CPS I are not a representative sample of the US population, the never smokers in this cohort had a total death rate that was close to that of US white never smokers. [19] Furthermore, the relative risks were based on comparisons within the cohort and should be valid.

Strengths of Study

CPS I has several important strengths: long established value as a prospective epidemiological study, large size, extensive baseline data on smoking and potential confounders, extensive follow up data, and excellent long term follow up. None of the other cohort studies on environmental tobacco smoke has more strength, and none has presented as many detailed results (see bmj.com). Considering these strengths as a whole, the CPS I cohort is one of the most valuable samples for studying the relation between environmental tobacco smoke and mortality.

Concern has been expressed that smoking status in spouses in 1959 does not accurately reflect total exposure to environmental tobacco smoke because there was so much exposure to non-residential environmental tobacco smoke at that time. The 1999 questionnaire showed that smoking status of spouses was directly related to a history of total exposure to environmental tobacco smoke It also showed that the extent of misclassification of exposure was not sufficient to obscure a true association between environmental tobacco smoke and coronary heart disease among women (see bmj.com).

Comparison with Other Studies

Our results for coronary heart disease and lung cancer are consistent with those of most of the other individual studies on environmental tobacco smoke, including the results for coronary heart disease and lung cancer in the full CPS I. Moreover, when our results are included in a meta-analysis of all results for coronary heart disease, the summary relative risks for current and ever exposure to environmental tobacco smoke are reduced to about 1.05, indicating a weak relation.

Widowhood was strongly correlated with smoking status of spouses, owing to the reduced survival of smokers. Since widowers have higher death rates than married people, controlling for widowhood would be expected to reduce the relative risks in this and other studies of smoking in spouses. The precise effect of widowhood due to smoking in spouses still needs to be determined, but it may partially explain the positive relative risks found in other cohorts.

Conclusion

The results of the California CPS I cohort do not support a causal relation between exposure to environmental tobacco smoke and tobacco related mortality, although they do not rule out a small effect. Given the limitations of the underlying data in this and the other studies of environmental tobacco smoke and the small size of the risk, it seems premature to conclude that environmental tobacco smoke causes death from coronary heart disease and lung cancer.

What Is Already Known on This Topic

- Exposure to environmental tobacco smoke is generally believed to increase the risk of coronary heart disease and lung cancer among never smokers by about 25%.

- This increase risk, based primarily on meta-analysis, is still controversial due to methodological problems.

In a large study of Californians followed for 40 years, environmental tobacco smoke was not associated with coronary heart disease or lung cancer mortality at any level of exposure.

These findings suggest that the effects of environmental tobacco smoke, particularly for coronary heart disease, are considerably smaller than generally believed.

Active cigarette smoking was confirmed as a strong, dose related risk factor for coronary heart disease, lung cancer, and chronic obstructive pulmonary disease.

What this Study Adds

In a large study of Californians followed for 40 years, environmental tobacco smoke was not associated with coronary heart disease or lung cancer mortality at any level of exposure.

These findings suggest that the effects of environmental tobacco smoke, particularly for coronary heart disease, are considerably smaller than generally believed.

Active cigarette smoking as confirmed was a strong, dose related risk factor for coronary heart disease, lung cancer, and chronic obstructive pulmonary disease.

A Vaccine Offers Protection Against Cervical Cancer

Barbara A. Bledrzycki

Barbara A. Bledrzycki is a research associate at Johns Hopkins School of Medicine in Baltimore. In this article she outlines the incidence of human papillomavirus (HPV). She notes that HPV infections are common, but in certain instances they can develop into cervical cancer. Bledrzycki discusses the development of the HPV vaccine, the Food and Drug Administration's approval of the Merck product, and the recommendation by the Centers for Disease Control and Prevention. The recommendation is not a mandate, she says, and each state must determine its own course. The HPV vaccine and the pap test are powerful tools to reduce cervical cancer rates around the world.

If we knew how to prevent cancer, would we? The Surgeon General issued a groundbreaking report in 1964 stating that cigarette smoking is known to cause cancer, but many still ignore the warning and continue to smoke. Smokers have many convincing rebuttals: Ciga-

SOURCE: Barbara A. Bledrzycki, "What If Preventing Cancer Is as Easy as Being Vaccinated?" *ONS News*, vol. 21, August 2006, pp. 9–10. Reproduced by permission.

rettes are physically and psychologically addictive, quitting is not easy, and nicotine replacement and will power often are not enough to facilitate quitting.

What if avoiding a carcinogen did not have those associated challenges? What if preventing one type of cancer was as easy as being vaccinated? And what if that type of cancer was the second most common worldwide cause of female cancer deaths? Would we use biotechnology to its full potential?

Incidence in the United States

According to the Centers for Disease Control and Prevention [CDC]

- Human papillomavirus (HPV) is the most common sexually transmitted disease (STD).
- 20 million men and women are infected.
- HPV is most common in people in their late teens and early 20s.
- 80% of women are infected by age 50.

Cervical cancer is unlike most cancers. It is a "rare complication of a very common infection." HPVs, a group of more than 100 viruses, are the major cause of cervical cancer. They also play a role in cancers of the anus, vulva, vagina, and penis and some cancers of the oropharynx. More than 30 types of HPV are known to be transmitted sexually, and half of them are considered to be high risk for the development of cervical cancer.

Healthcare professionals have a unique opportunity to detect and prevent cervical cancer because it has a well-defined precancerous state, the cervix is accessible for screening and treatment, and the cause (HPV) is known. Although HPV infection may last for months or years, most people are able to clear the infection through the immune system.

Women are most at risk for high-grade cervical dysplasia when an HPV type 16 or 18 infection lasts for more than six months. Left untreated, the persistent dsyplasia can transform into a lethal cancer.

Research and Development

Two major pharmaceutical companies, GlaxoSmithKline and Merck & Co., Inc., were competing to be the first to get an HPV vaccine to market. GlaxoSmithKline's HPV vaccine, Ceravix™, demonstrated 100% efficacy against the precancerous lesions associated with HPV types 16 and 18 for 4.5 years. Merck's HPV vaccine, Gardasil®, protects against cervical cancer, precancerous lesions, and cervical dysplasia associated with types 16 and 18. In addition, Gardasil protects against the HPV types that are responsible for 90% of genital warts, types 6 and 11.

> **FAST FACT**
>
> Twenty percent of cancers worldwide are caused by chronic infections such as hepatitis B, human papillomavirus, and others.

Both HPV vaccines were administered in research studies as three intramuscular injections over a six-month period. The U.S. Food and Drug Administration (FDA) granted unanimous approval of Merck's Gardasil investigational new drug application on June 8, 2006. Ceravix is still under the FDA's review.

National Recommendations

"Today is a historic day," said Anne Schuchat, MD, director of CDC's National Center for Immunizations and Respiratory Diseases, at a June 29 press conference announcing that the United States was the first country to make a national vaccination recommendation for HPV. The announcement was made shortly after the Advisory Committee of Immunization Practices (ACIP) voted unanimously to recommend that Gardasil be given to 11–12-year-old girls. Although the 11–12 age group will be targeted, ACIP emphasized that the vaccine can be used until age 26 and, at healthcare providers' discretion, as early as age 9.

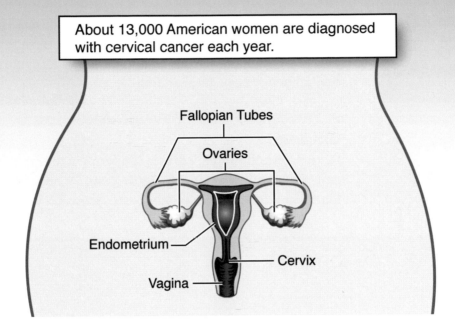

About 13,000 American women are diagnosed with cervical cancer each year.

Fallopian Tubes

Ovaries

Endometrium

Cervix

Vagina

After FDA approval, ACIP considers the efficacy, safety, and cost effectiveness of a vaccine before it makes its recommendations. ACIP has resolved that the HPV vaccine be included in the Vaccination for Children (VFC) Program, a national effort that provides free immunizations to children who are Medicaid eligible, uninsured, underinsured, or Native American. The guidelines became official when published in the CDC's *Morbidity and Mortality Weekly Report.*

Keep in mind that the recommendations are not national mandates. Each state independently determines its own vaccination mandates for school-age children. The VFC program provides access to the HPV vaccine for some children. Health insurance providers customarily consider the recommendations of the ACIP when deciding their coverage benefits. Access for uninsured or low-income adults will be strengthened by Merck's assistance program.

"About 40%–45% of the U.S. child population is included in the VFC," said Lance Rodewald, MD, of the Immunization Services Division. He indicated that, usually within the first year of a recommendation being issued, about a fifth of the population will be vaccinated; after several years, expectations are for 90% coverage.

A Potential Yet Preventable Global Epidemic

In the United States, cervical cancer once was a major cause of cancer deaths. But now, mainly because of the Papanicolaou (Pap) test, death rates from cervical cancer

Dr. Ian Frazer, the inventor of Gardasil, injects the vaccine into a patient in Sydney, Australia. Gardasil protects against HPV, a virus which can cause cervical cancer. (AP Images)

continue to decline by almost 4% per year. In developing countries, cervical cancer is responsible for 15% of all cancer deaths, yet those countries have only 5% of the world's cancer resources available. Access to testing and treatments is why 70% of women with cervical cancer in the United States live and why 59% of women with cervical cancer in developing countries die.

Research already is under way to develop advanced HPV vaccine technology. Perhaps therapeutic vaccines can be developed to prevent cervical cancer after HPV exposure or after the development of cervical dysplasia, carcinoma in situ, or invasive cervical cancer. Perhaps a more feasible delivery system for distribution of the HPV vaccine can reduce the cost and increase use in developing countries.

About 75% of the 4.7 million abnormal Pap tests that require costly follow-up every year are related to HPV. Merck estimated that five billion healthcare dollars are spent in the United States annually on HPV-related disease. In addition to expenses, high stress levels associated with repeated testing and the ever-present threat of cervical cancer may be eliminated with the HPV vaccine.

Even though HPV is an STD [sexually transmitted disease] shared between the sexes, the HPV vaccine is targeted only to females, the sex at risk for the deadly sequela of HPV: cervical cancer. HPV vaccination of females could offer herd immunity to men and women.

A Cervical Cancer Vaccine Poses Problems to Some

Maryann Napoli

Maryann Napoli is the associate director of the Center for Medical Consumers, a nonprofit organization which provides science-based medical information to the public. In this article she raises questions about the HPV vaccine. She notes that most mass vaccinations have been for diseases that are widespread and fatal to many people. HPV is widespread, but Napoli argues that the low death rate from cervical cancer does not justify mass inoculations. She has serious concerns about the clinical tests as well. Napoli questions the testing process, since both vaccine and placebo contained aluminum, a metal that causes inflammation and brain cell death. She also questions why so few girls participated in the tests.

The cervical cancer vaccine raises concerns that did not show up in the news coverage about its approval last summer. Usually mass vaccinations are

SOURCE: Maryann Napoli, "New Cervical Cancer Vaccine Should Not Be Mandatory," *Health Facts*, November 2006, p. 1. Maryann Napoli, Center for Medical Consumers. Copyright © 2006. Reproduced by permission.

advised for diseases with a high rate of death and/or disability, but cervical cancer doesn't come close to meeting those criteria. And most important: Is it safe to vaccinate all girls for a disease that afflicts only 9,710 American women yearly and causes 3,700 deaths? The answer might be yes, if the vaccine is risk-free. But the nation's leading vaccine safety organization raises some serious reservations.

Those reservations were ignored last summer when the Centers for Disease Control and Prevention Advisory Committee on Immunization Practices voted to recommend that all 11- to 12-year-old girls receive the human papillomavirus (HPV) vaccine called Gardasil. This is a major step toward making the vaccine mandatory—at an age well before girls are likely to become sexually active.

Only one company, Merck, makes the HPV vaccine, which is given in three injections over six months and will cost $360. Merck says its trials proved Gardasil is "100% effective in preventing HPV infection in those who do not already have HPV with strains 16 and 18, which together cause about 70% of all cases of cervical cancer."

Cervical Cancer Vaccine May Not Be Needed

These Merck-sponsored trials were submitted to the FDA, and Gardasil was approved. But Barbara Loe Fisher, an advocate for vaccine-safety studies and the president of the National Vaccine Information Center, questions the need for a cervical cancer vaccine given the availability of the Pap test, which she believes has greatly reduced the incidence of the disease. She also sees methodological flaws and major deficiencies in what has been reported to the public about HPV disease and the vaccine.

"Most people who have sex will have experience with HPV, but the majority will clear it from the body and go on to have healthy lives. Only a tiny percentage will have persistent HPV infection and will experience changes over a long period of time that will lead to cancer. On the list of cancers that kill, this is at the bottom," she said, referring to U.S. women, as opposed to those in developing countries where cervical cancer deaths are far more common.

As a former member of the FDA Vaccines and Related Biologic Products Advisory Committee, Fisher has considerable experience analyzing the lengthy documents submitted by the vaccine companies to the FDA, as well as the agency's own review of company-sponsored trials. Fisher's safety concerns center on the type of placebo Merck used in the Gardasil trials. "A true placebo would

In 2007 state representative Dennis Bonnen successfully worked to change the law so that sixth-grade girls in Texas would no longer be required to take the HPV vaccine. **(AP Images)**

be a saline solution—something that is innocuous and has no potential to cause a reaction on its own," she said, referring to the injection given study participants who were assigned to the control group against which Gardasil was compared.

Merck's Clinical Test Raises Questions

FAST FACT

According to a Canadian study, most women who are infected with even "high risk" HPV will not develop cervical cancer.

Instead, Merck used a solution that contained aluminum, Fisher explained, and neither the company nor the FDA has publicly disclosed the amount used in the solution. "Aluminum is used as an adjuvant in many vaccines to boost the potency of the vaccine," she continued, "and though it has been in vaccines for decades, it has never been tested in clinical trials to see whether it is safe.

"We know from animal and human biological mechanism research that aluminum can cause inflammation and brain cell death. Putting it in the placebo [in a clinical trial] violates the principle of the scientific method when trying to ascertain truth," said Fisher. "To make matters worse, aluminum is also in the Gardasil vaccine which makes it difficult to tell whether the many adverse events reported in the trials were due to the aluminum-containing placebo or the Gardasil," she explained, referring to the well-documented fact that adverse events will show up in all clinical trial participants, even those given an inactive placebo.

Why would the FDA overlook this potential for confounding trial results? "The FDA has become partners with the vaccine manufacturers in fast-tracking these vaccines and in the process, the precautionary principle has been thrown out," Fisher responded, adding that most health problems occurring in vaccine trials are often dismissed. "The companies tend to write them off as unassociated with the vaccine."

Natural History of HPV Infection

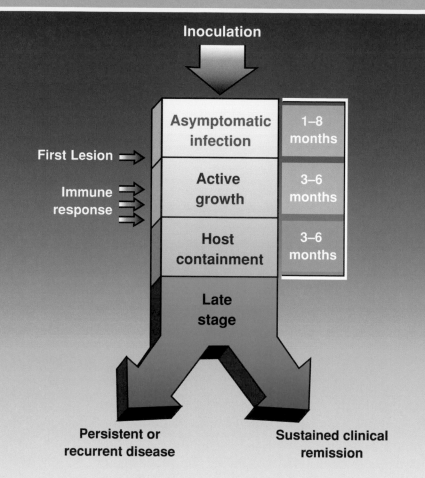

Inoculation

Asymptomatic infection	1–8 months	
First Lesion → Active growth	3–6 months	
Immune response → Host containment	3–6 months	

Late stage

Persistent or recurrent disease Sustained clinical remission

Source: American Society for Colposcopy and Cervical Pathology, *Modern Colposcopy: A Practical Approach,* 1999.

Questions About the Clinical Test

Another disturbing aspect of the Gardasil approval process involves the small number of young girls who actually participated in Merck's trials. The company states that its trials had more than 20,000 participants, but it would take considerable time to [pore] through the numerous pages of documentation in order to separate the adults from the children. A *New York Times* reporter did just that last July. Roni Rabin, who is also the mother of a nine-year-old girl, found that fewer than

1,200 participants were under 16 and the younger girls were followed for only 18 months.

This is not the first time that young children will be vaccinated for a sexually transmitted disease. The first in a series of hepatitis B vaccine shots is administered at birth. Few would object to hepatitis B vaccinations for infants born of women infected with hepatitis B. But there were plenty of objections, even among pediatricians, when the hepatitis B vaccine became mandatory for a disease most likely to afflict prostitutes, injection-drug users, and men who have sex with men.

Putting Gardasil on the ever-expanding schedule of childhood vaccinations might bring another round of objections, now that states like Michigan are moving toward making the cervical cancer vaccine mandatory. Yet Fisher notes a sea change in the public's attitude toward vaccines and drugs, "People want the right to make informed health choices, and vaccination is the toughest area to make a choice."

Alternative Treatments for Cancer Work

Kerry Hughes

Kerry Hughes is a writer for *Prepared Foods* magazine. In this article he examines the role of food and supplements to help reduce cancer risks. He notes that factors such as not smoking, eating right, and exercising are common recommendations. He also examines a selection of herbal supplements as well as vitamins and minerals, and concludes that healthy eating combined with alternative supplements is a strong defense against cancer.

According to the American Cancer Society (Atlanta), approximately 35% of all cancer deaths in the U.S. can be prevented by dietary means. Scientific evidence shows that properly balancing fruits, vegetables, dietary fiber, antioxidants, vitamins, minerals and certain dietary supplements protects our health.

A good diet often translates into good health. One type of cancer that is most associated with a diet poor in fiber

SOURCE: Kerry Hughes, "Ingredients to Reduce Cancer Risks," *Prepared Foods*, January 2007, p. NS3. Copyright © 2007 BNP Media. Reproduced by permission.

is colorectal cancer. Colon and rectal cancers are the number two cancer killers in the U.S. Certain lifestyle habits have been associated with a higher risk of these diseases:

- A diet high in red meat, or heavily processed or cooked meat,
- A lack of exercise,
- Obesity and
- Cigarette smoking.

There are a number of things that can be done to reduce the risk of colorectal cancer, including eating more fruits, vegetables and dietary fiber, increasing exercise, maintaining a healthy weight and getting regular health screenings. According to Isaac Eliaz, M.D., a cancer specialist who uses both Western and Eastern approaches to medicine, of Amitabha Medical Clinic and Healing Center (Sebastopol, Calif.), supplements of folic acid, vitamin D3 and calcium also may have a beneficial effect.

> **FAST FACT**
>
> According to the Mayo Clinic, acupuncture has been effective in treating pain and nausea in some cancer patients.

Research shows that many of the recommendations addressing colon cancer can be used to reduce risk of other types, as well. Particularly, eating plenty of fruits and vegetables is helpful, while diets high in fat are linked to an increased risk of breast, colon, prostate and, possibly, pancreatic, ovarian and endometrial cancers. . . .

Upping Antioxidants

Antioxidants protect cells and their contents (including DNA) from oxidative damage that could lead to cancer. Antioxidants are a large category with numerous compounds, such as the bioflavonoid pigments found in plants and green tea; the vitamins A, C and E; and minerals such as selenium.

In a review of the literature on cancer risk reduction by antioxidants, [J.B.] Block and [S.] Evans concluded that "antioxidants and other nutritional supplements would appear to have potential for the most profound benefit in reducing the risk of certain identified diseases, such as cancer, in these populations where adequate an-

Reducing the Risk: Information on the Web

www.dreliaz.com/about.php
Ask Dr. Eliaz.com

http://familydoctor.org
Food recommendations to reduce cancer risk

http://seer.cancer.gov/publications/raterisk/risks73.html
National Cancer Institute's risk factors

www.cancer.gov/newscenter/pressreleases/tea
National Cancer Institute fact sheet, "Tea and Cancer Prevention"

www.nalusda.gov/fnic/dga/dguide95.html
Hypertext version of FDA's Dietary Guidelines for Americans

www.preventcancer.org
Cancer Research Foundation of America

www.aicr.org
American Institute for Cancer Research

www.aicr.org
The Diet and Cancer Link

http://wwwicic.nci.nih.gov/cancertopics
National Cancer Institute; Info. for health professionals, statistics, journals

www.hopkinskimmelcancercenter.org
Johns Hopkins Oncology Center

Source: BNP Media.

tioxidant plasma levels and intake are not achieved through appropriate dietary sources." Among the diseases reduced by antioxidant supplementation were prostate, cervical, oral, gastric, esophageal, skin and lung cancers. Some commercially available compounds have carefully been researched for their benefits in this area.

For instance, lycopene, the pigment molecule and antioxidant present in tomatoes, has been found to reduce the size of fibroid tumors in animal studies. Several other studies also have found that lycopene may prevent or even slow the progression of certain cancers, including prostate cancer.

Recent research has shown that lycopene helps to stimulate production of phase II detoxification enzymes that are regulated by an "antioxidant response element" or ARE.

Vitamins Help Protect Against Cancer

Everyone's old favorite, vitamin C, has been found to protect against cancers of the esophagus, oral cavity, stomach and, possibly, the pancreas, rectum and cervix.

Vitamin A and carotenoids have been associated with reducing the risk of certain cancers, especially lung cancer. Studies including smokers have demonstrated that those consuming carotenoid-rich foods had a reduced risk of lung cancer.

Vitamin D deficiency has been coined the new epidemic among adolescents and is due, in part, to a decrease in milk consumption and exposure to sunlight. Among the potential dangers and results of this deficiency are various bone problems and the development of certain types of cancers.

Recently, at least one study showed that foods rich in vitamin E, such as olive oil, nuts, spinach and mustard greens cut the risk of bladder cancer in half. This disease is the fourth leading cancer killer among men. Prior studies have been conducted on alpha-tocopherol in smokers' diets, and its ability to protect against lung and other cancers. Vitamin E's role in cancer-prevention is not yet thoroughly established in that there also have been many studies that show it has no effect, making vitamin E's role in cancer unclear.

Minerals to Tea

One of the most notable minerals for cancer prevention is selenium, which also is an antioxidant. The supplementation of 200mcg/day of selenium for people living in the U.S. in areas of selenium-deficient soil has resulted in an overall cancer mortality rate reduction of 21%, with prostate cancer being reduced by 65%.

Calcium also may be an important cancer-preventative in the diet. The consumption of 700mg of calcium daily has been found to significantly reduce the risk of developing colon cancer for both men and women.

Women with this level of calcium consumption had a 27% reduction in distal colon cancer, and men had a 42% reduction. Although milk often is touted as the best food source of calcium, even better sources are turnip greens, mustard greens, collard greens and tofu (processed with calcium).

One of the most widely consumed beverages on a worldwide basis, tea has been the subject of numerous studies for its chemopreventive benefits. Tea contains the antioxidant catechin, which is thought to be a prime chemopreventive compound. In earlier animal studies, catechins reduced the size of tumors and scavenged oxidants before they damaged the cells. Clinical studies in humans thus far have been inconclusive; however, this is probably due to variances in the diets, populations and environments studied. Tea is implicated in the prevention of numerous types of cancers, and the National Cancer Institute (Bethesda, Md.) is investigating it for its therapeutic and preventative ability in cancers, including skin cancer.

Soy Protein and Genistein

The FDA is reviewing a petition for a health claim suggesting soy protein–based foods are able to reduce the risk of certain cancers, including those of the breast, prostate, uterus and colon, as these are the areas in which clinical research has found soy to be most effective.

In some exciting new research on the benefits of men eating soy products, it has been found that diets high in soy may prevent both baldness and prostate cancer. Soy compounds can be converted into a hormone-like compound called equol. Equol is a natural and powerful

Thomas McCloud gives reporters a tour of the Natural Products Support Group. At this facility the National Cancer Institute studies fungus, marine creatures, and other life forms in search of naturally occuring anticancer substances. **(AP Images)**

blocker of dihydrotestosterone, or DHT. DHT is known to promote male-pattern baldness, as well as prostate cancer growth. More research indicates genistein-concentrated polysaccharide can reduce the levels of prostate-specific antigen (PSA) in "watchful waiting" patients. PSA often is used as an indicator of prostate cancer growth and metastasis.

Regularly eating soya-rich foods recently has been reported to also decrease the risk of uterine cancer in women. As soya-rich foods previously have been linked to reducing breast cancer, these results are exciting because they add to the mounting evidence that isoflavones' estrogen effect, including genistein, may be beneficial in fighting heart disease and cancer.

Other Supplements and the Integrative Approach

A promising supplement and food ingredient for cancer prevention and treatment is Modified Citrus Pectin (MCP). MCP is a type of citrus pectin specially processed to limit the size of the pectin molecules, allowing them to be absorbed easily into the bloodstream. In clinical trials, MCP reduces the size of tumors, prevents metastasis and reduces any blood capillary formation in tumors, halting the development of cancer. MCP also has shown promising results as a gentle chelator of heavy metals. According to Isaac Eliaz, M.D., MCP plays an important adjunctive role in cancer, as heavy metal toxicity often is linked to the cause or acceleration of pathological illnesses, such as cancer.

Eliaz also has respect for less conventional, but very traditional approaches. Eliaz says that medicinal mushrooms are important in his treatment of cancer patients. "For my patients, I use a mixture of the ancient medicinal mushrooms that have been used for millennia in traditional Chinese medicine. They act as immune enhancers, and show powerful anti-cancer properties." Most of these medicinal mushrooms also are considered foods, and are being confirmed by science to bolster the immune system.

He adds that, "Prevention and treatment of cancer requires an integrative approach. Simple lifestyle changes: regular walking, proper restorative sleep, hydration with a good water source, and a healthy diet, can have long-term and far-reaching benefits. When those simple lifestyle changes are combined with conventional therapies, they make both conventional and alternative therapies more effective and enhance the healing potential."

Alternative Treatments for Cancer Do Not Work

Ben Goldacre

Ben Goldacre writes "Bad Science," a feature of the *Guardian* newspaper. He also has a book and Web site by the same name. In this article Goldacre looks at the claims made by the alternative therapy industry and concludes that they are without substance. Because this industry does not subject their products to the same level of testing as does the medical community, he concludes that those treatments cannot be proven to work.

I t can sometimes seem like there are two competing ways to make a decision about any complex matter of evidence-based medicine. One is to purchase and digest *How To Read A Paper* by Professor Trisha Greenhalgh, and then find, read, and critically appraise every published academic study independently and in full for

SOURCE: Ben Goldacre, "Food for Thought on Alternative Therapy," *Guardian*, June 24, 2006, p. 14. Copyright © 2006 Guardian Newspapers Limited. Reproduced by permission of Guardian News Service, LTD.

yourself. The other more common method is to rely on "experts", or what I like to call "prejudice".

But there is a third way: what we might call "evidence-based prejudice". I can't possibly debunk every single alternative therapy column you will ever read: but if I could show that their single most popular claim has no foundation, then you could safely ignore everything else they say, thus saving valuable brain energy, and creating time to write bestselling novels and eradicate world poverty.

And so to antioxidants. The basic claim of the alternative therapy industry is as follows: free radicals in the body are bad, but antioxidants neutralise free radicals;

In 2005 Flavonoid Sciences and 28 other manufacturers of cherry-based dietary supplements were warned by the FDA that they must stop making unproven claims about the health benefits of antioxidants in their products. (**AP Images**)

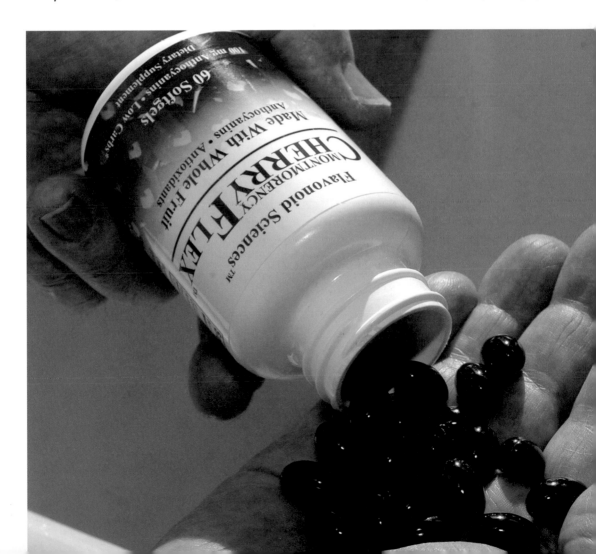

people who eat vegetables with antioxidants in them live longer, therefore antioxidant tablets are good.

Now this "free-radicals-bad, antioxidants-good" morality tale looks great on paper. But if you're going to read a biochemistry textbook and pull bits out at random, you can prove anything you like. For example, my phagocytic cells build a wall around invading pathogens and then use free radicals—among other things—to kill the bacteria off, before the bacteria kill me. They're probably doing it right now. So do I need free radical supplements to help me fight infections? Sounds plausible. You can see, now, how I could make some serious money if I ever turned to the dark side.

Of course, the "antioxidants good" story didn't come entirely out of the blue: it came, like almost all the evidence on diet and health, from observational studies. People who eat well, with plenty of fruit and vegetables in their diet, tend to live longer, healthier lives.

But these are observational studies, not intervention studies. These are not studies where you take a few thousand people and make them eat salad. These are surveys, looking at people who, like me, already have healthy diets and lifestyles. But it's not just the antioxidants in rocket salad.

So what happens, then, when people do big studies, forcing people to eat salad? Well, it's not an easy thing to do, if only because it's difficult to get people to eat what you tell them, and measure what they eat, and check if they're truthful, and so on. The Multiple Risk Factor Intervention Trial in the 1970s was probably the single biggest medical project. It took 12,866 men, advised them, monitored them, cajoled them, persuaded them, followed them up for a decade, and found little benefit from dietary change. Intervention trials for diet have continued, since then, to produce negative results.

> **FAST FACT**
>
> "Megavitamin diets" can interfere with cancer treatment.

The Risks of Alternative Medicines

Product	Alias	Side Effects
Aconite	*Monkshood Wolfbane*	Nausea, vomiting, neuromuscular weakness, seizures, coma Cardiac effects—bradycardia, arrhythmia, and hypotension
Chaparral Tea		Liver failure
Chomper		May be contaminated with digitalis, a type of flower that can be toxic
Lobelia		Vomiting, coma, tachycardia, respiratory distress
Ma Huang	*Ephedra*	Hypertension, heart attack, stroke, arrhythmias, headaches, seizures, tremors, anxiety, hallucinations
Pennyroyal		Liver and renal failure, nausea, vomiting, abdominal pain, shock Alterations in mental status (delirium, confusion, agitation, seizures)
Plantain Leaf		May be contaminated with digitalis
Yohimbe		Seizures, renal failure

Source: Barrie R. Cassileth, *The Alternative Medicine Handbook*, 1998, and Ronald B. Mack, "Something Wicked this Way Comes," *Contemporary Pediatrics*, 1998, pp. 49–64.

But what about vitamin tablets? They're easy to study, in the sense that it's easy to take a tablet—easier than changing your whole food lifestyle—easy to find a placebo control for, and so on. And there have been innumerable studies, and systematic reviews of those studies, and meta-analyses of those studies, and they have found no benefit for antioxidants. A meta-analysis—a mathematical combination of lots of smaller studies to give one larger and more accurate answer—of 15 studies, a total of over 200,000 patients, being followed up for between one and 12 years, found no benefit for cardiovascular outcomes. The current Cochrane review on antioxidants and bowel cancer had just as many patients, and again found no benefit for the pills.

That must be the single most prevalent claim of the alternative therapy industry: and it is in stark contradiction of the experience of hundreds of thousands of individuals who have been carefully studied in these trials, examining advice from the alternative therapy industry. If they can't get that one thing right, why listen to them on anything else?

Marijuana Can Ease the Side Effects of Chemotherapy

The Economist

The medical use of marijuana continues to stir up controversy, according to the editors of the *Economist*, a British business magazine. Even though the Food and Drug Administration asserts that marijuana has no medical use, the *Economist* article cites conflicting opinions. One U.S. study performed by a division of the National Academy of Sciences found evidence that limited marijuana use was beneficial. Some doctors, the article states, have advised their patients suffering from cancer and other diseases to get marijuana on the black market. Proponents of marijuana use say that it can suppress nausea and vomiting experienced by many cancer patients undergoing chemotherapy. The article cites the need for more research to determine the best way to use marijuana's active ingredients.

If cannabis were unknown, and bioprospectors were suddenly to find it in some remote mountain crevice, its discovery would no doubt be hailed as a medical

SOURCE: *The Economist*, "Reefer Madness," vol. 379, April 29, 2006, pp. 83–84. Copyright © The Economist Newspaper Ltd. All rights reserved. Republished with permission of The Economist Newspaper Ltd., conveyed through Copyright Clearance Center, Inc.

Christopher Campbell displays a roll of medical marijuana, which he takes for relief from pain and nausea caused by his cancer. (AP Images)

breakthrough. Scientists would praise its potential for treating everything from pain to cancer, and marvel at its rich pharmacopoeia—many of whose chemicals mimic vital molecules in the human body. In reality, cannabis has been with humanity for thousands of years and is considered by many governments (notably America's) to be a dangerous drug without utility. Any suggestion that the plant might be medically useful is politically controversial, whatever the science says. It is in this context that, on April 20th [2006], America's Food and Drug Administration (FDA) issued a statement saying that smoked marijuana has no accepted medical use in treatment in the United States.

The statement is curious in a number of ways. For one thing, it overlooks a report made in 1999 by the Institute of Medicine (IOM), part of the National Academy of Sciences, which came to a different conclusion. John Benson, a professor of medicine at the University of Nebraska who co-chaired the committee that drew up the report, found some sound scientific information that supports the medical use of marijuana for certain patients for short periods—even for smoked marijuana.

This is important, because one of the objections to marijuana is that, when burned, its smoke contains many of the harmful things found in tobacco smoke, such as carcinogenic tar, cyanide and carbon monoxide. Yet the IOM report supports what some patients suffering from multiple sclerosis, AIDS and cancer—and their doctors—have known for a long time. This is that the drug gives them medicinal benefits over and above the medications they are already receiving, and despite the fact that the smoke has risks. That is probably why several studies show that many doctors recommend smoking cannabis to their patients, even though they are unable to prescribe it. Patients then turn to the black market for their supply.

Medical Marijuana Has Been Used for Centuries

Another reason the FDA statement is odd is that it seems to lack common sense. Cannabis has been used as a medicinal plant for millennia. In fact, the American government actually supplied cannabis as a medicine for some time, before the scheme was shut down in the early 1990s. Today, cannabis is used all over the world, despite its illegality, to relieve pain and anxiety, to aid sleep, and to prevent seizures and muscle spasms. For example, two of its long-advocated benefits are that it suppresses vomiting and enhances appetite—qualities that AIDS patients and those on anti-cancer chemotherapy find useful. So useful, in fact, that the FDA has licensed a drug called Marinol, a synthetic version of one of the active ingredients of marijuana—delta-9-tetrahydrocannabinol (THC). Unfortunately, many users of Marinol complain that it gets them high (which isn't what they actually want) and is not nearly as effective, nor cheap, as the real weed itself.

This may be because Marinol is ingested into the stomach, meaning that it is metabolised before being absorbed. Or it may be because the medicinal benefits of cannabis come from the synergistic effect of the multiplicity of chemicals it contains.

Marijuana Has Many Ingredients that May Have Medical Applications

THC is the best known active ingredient of cannabis, but by no means the only one. At the last count, marijuana was known to contain nearly 70 different cannabinoids, as THC and its cousins are collectively known. These chemicals activate receptor molecules in the human body, particularly the cannabinoid receptors on the surfaces of some nerve cells in the brain, and stimulate changes in biochemical activity. But the details often remain vague—in particular, the details of which molecules are having which clinical effects.

More clinical research would help. In particular, the breeding of different varieties of cannabis, with different mixtures of cannabinoids, would enable researchers to find out whether one variety works better for, say, multiple sclerosis-related spasticity while another works for AIDS-related nerve pain. However, in the United States, this kind of work has been inhibited by marijuana's illegality and the unwillingness of the Drug Enforcement Administration (DEA) to license researchers to grow it for research.

The Government Is Blocking Marijuana Research

Since 2001, for example, Lyle Craker, a researcher at the University of Massachusetts, has been trying to obtain a licence from the DEA to grow cannabis for use in clinical research. After years of prevarication, and pressure on

States Legalizing Medical Marijuana

Medical Marijuana Is Accepted

Medical Marijuana Is Rejected

Considering Medical Marijuana

Special Circumstances

VT 2004
ME 1999
WA 1998
MT 2004
OR 1998
RI 2006
SD 2006
NV 2000
CO 2000
CA 1996
MD 2003
MD has an affirmative defense for medical users.
AZ 1996
NM 2007

AZ passed medical marijuana but could not enact the law as it required a doctor's prescription, in violation of federal law.

AK 1998

DC 1998
DC passed medical marijuana but was blocked by Congress from enacting the law.

HI 2000

Source: Oregon NORML.

the DEA to make a decision, Dr Craker's application was turned down in 2004. Today, the saga continues and a DEA judge (who presides over a quasi-judicial process within the agency) is hearing an appeal, which could come to a close the summer of 2006. Dr Craker says that his situation is like that described in Joseph Heller's novel, *Catch 22*. "We can say that this has no medical benefit because no tests have been done, and then we refuse to let you do any tests. The US has gotten into a bind, it has made cannabis out to be such a villain that people blindly say 'no.'"

Anjuli Verma, the advocacy director of the American Civil Liberties Union (ACLU), a group helping Dr Craker fight his appeal, says that even if the DEA judge rules in their favour, the agency's chief administrator can still decide whether to allow the application. And, as she points out, the DEA is a political organisation charged with enforcing the drug laws. So, she says, the ACLU is in this for the long haul, and is already prepared for another appeal—one that would be heard in a federal court in the normal judicial system.

Ms Verma's view of the FDA's statement is that other arms of government are putting pressure on the agency to make a public pronouncement that conforms with drug ideology as promulgated by the White House, the DEA and a number of vocal anti-cannabis congressmen. In particular, the federal government has been rattled in recent years by the fact that eleven states have passed laws allowing the medical use of marijuana. In this context it is notable that the FDA's statement emphasises that it is smoked marijuana which has not gone through the process necessary to make it a prescription drug. (Nor would it be likely to, with all of the harmful things in the smoke.) The statement's emphasis on smoked marijuana is important because it leaves the door open for the agency to approve other methods of delivery.

Other Countries Conduct Marijuana Research

Donald Abrams, a professor of clinical medicine at the University of California, San Francisco, has been working on one such option. He is allowed by the National Institute on Drug Abuse (the only legal supplier of cannabis in the United States) to do research on a German nebuliser that heats cannabis to the point of vaporisation, where it releases its cannabinoids without any of the smoke of a spliff, and with fewer carcinogens.

That is encouraging. But it does not address the wider question of which cannabinoids are doing what. For that, researchers need to be able to do their own plant-breeding programmes.

In America, this is impossible. But it is happening in other countries. In 1997, for example, the British government asked Geoffrey Guy, the executive chairman and founder of GW Pharmaceuticals, to come up with a programme to develop cannabis into a pharmaceutical product.

In the intervening years, GW has assembled a "library" of more than 300 varieties of cannabis, and obtained plant-breeder's rights on between 30 and 40 of these. It has found the genes that control cannabinoid production and can specify within strict limits the seven or eight cannabinoids it is most interested in. And it knows how to crossbreed its strains to get the mixtures it wants.

> **FAST FACT**
>
> In a 2002 CNN poll, 80 percent of respondents favored the use of marijuana for medical purposes.

Nor is this knowledge merely academic. Last year [2005], GW gained approval in Canada for the use of its first drug, Sativex, which is an extract of cannabis sprayed under the tongue that is designed for the relief of neuropathic pain in multiple sclerosis. Sativex is also available to a more limited degree in Spain and Britain, and is in clinical trials for other uses, such as relieving the pain of rheumatoid arthritis.

At the start of this year [2006], the company made the first step towards gaining regulatory approval for Sativex in America when the FDA accepted it as a legitimate candidate for clinical trials. But there is still a long way to go.

And that delay raises an important point. Once available, a well-formulated and scientifically tested drug should knock a herbal medicine into a cocked hat. No one would argue for chewing willow bark when aspirin is available. But, in the meantime, there is unmet medical need that, as the IOM report pointed out, could easily and cheaply be met—if the American government cared more about suffering and less about posturing.

Marijuana Has No Medical Application

David Evans

David Evans writes for the Drug Prevention Networks of the Americas, a coalition of private organizations dedicated to creating drug-free schools in North and South America. Evans reviews the Food and Drug Administration's ruling that medical marijuana has no medical benefit. Evans argues that the FDA's position is correct: Marijuana use has serious health side effects.

O ver the last three decades, the advocates of drug-legalization have employed a number of political and legal strategies to legitimize smoking marijuana. One of their strategies is to promote smoked marijuana as "medicine." They provide misleading and inaccurate information that smoking marijuana can help ill people.

SOURCE: David Evans, "Don't Legalize 'Medical Use' of Smoked Marijuana," The Drug Free Schools Coalition. Reproduced by permission of the author.

The federal Food and Drug Administration (FDA) will not approve smoked marijuana as medicine. In an attempt to by-pass the FDA, the legalizers have attempted to legitimize smoking marijuana as medicine by trying to pass state ballot initiatives and statutes. This seriously threatens the FDA process of approving safe medicines. It creates an atmosphere of medicine by popular vote, rather than the rigorous scientific and medical process that all medicines must currently undergo.

The U.S. Supreme Court in the case of *U.S. v. Oakland Cannabis Buyers Coop.*, reviewed such a California

These protestors gathered outside Los Angeles City Hall on January 22, 2007, to complain about recent federal raids on medical marijuana facilities in the area. **(AP Images)**

ballot initiative and unanimously decided that smoked marijuana has "no currently accepted medical use at all." In deciding that smoked crude marijuana is not a medicine, the court upheld the FDA drug approval process.

Before the development of modern pharmaceutical science, the field of medicine was fraught with potions. There were as many anecdotal stories about these potions as there are today about smoked marijuana. Many people were convinced that these potions helped them. However, many of these potions were absolutely useless, or conversely were harmful to unsuspecting ill people. Thus evolved our current FDA drug approval process. The FDA process has protected us for 100 years. It is dangerous to undermine it.

Smoked marijuana as medicine has also been rejected by the American Medical Association, the National Multiple Sclerosis Society, the American Glaucoma Society, the American Academy of Ophthalmology and the American Cancer Society. Recently, the federal Institute of Medicine also conducted research on this issue and they see "little future in smoked marijuana as a medicine." There are good reasons why they reject smoked marijuana.

> ## FAST FACT
>
> Marijuana contains the same cancer-causing compounds as tobacco.

FDA-Approved Medicines Provide Safe Alternatives to Smoked Marijuana

The major reason to reject crude smoked marijuana is that numerous safe and effective FDA approved medicines are available for all the conditions that smoked marijuana supposedly helps. This includes a drug in liquid form that is derived from the marijuana plant and was approved by the FDA for treating nausea in cancer patients and wasting in AIDS patients. The drug's generic name is dronabinol with the trade name of Marinol.

The respiratory damage associated with marijuana smoke speaks against inhaling marijuana as a medicine.

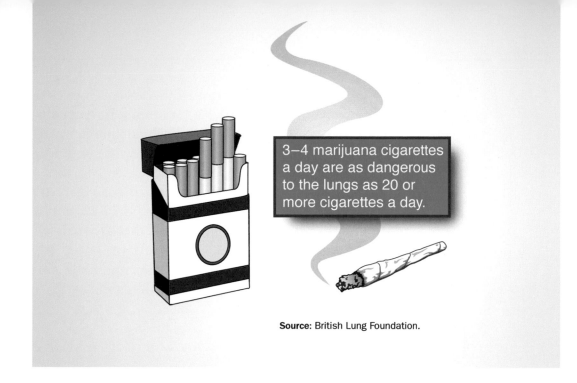

3–4 marijuana cigarettes a day are as dangerous to the lungs as 20 or more cigarettes a day.

Source: British Lung Foundation.

Smoked marijuana is associated with higher concentrations of tar, carbon monoxide, and carcinogens than even cigarette smoke.

One of the earliest findings in marijuana research was the effect on the various bodily immune functions. Cellular immunity is impaired, pulmonary immunity is impaired, and the impaired ability to fight infection is now documented in humans. It is clear that use of smoked marijuana bears substantial health risks especially for people at high risk for infection and immune suppression such as AIDS and cancer chemotherapy patients.

Marijuana Poses a Serious Risk for Abuse

Scientific literature shows that use of marijuana is a major risk factor in the development of addiction and drug use among our school children. The efforts to confuse the public about marijuana have contributed to the drop in school children's perception of marijuana's harm which results in marijuana and other drug use among school children. Of the nearly 182,000 kids in treatment today, 48% were admitted for abuse or addiction to marijuana while only 19.3% for alcohol and 2.9% for cocaine, 2.4% for methamphetamine and 2.3% for heroin. It is no coincidence that those states with medical marijuana initiatives have among the highest levels of drug use and drug addiction.

It is not compassionate to give marijuana cigarettes to sick people. They may mistakenly choose to smoke marijuana instead of using medicines that are truly effective. Crude smoked marijuana contains some 400 chemicals. Smoked marijuana, an impure and toxic substance, has no place in our medicine cabinets.

CHAPTER 3

Personal Perspectives on Cancer

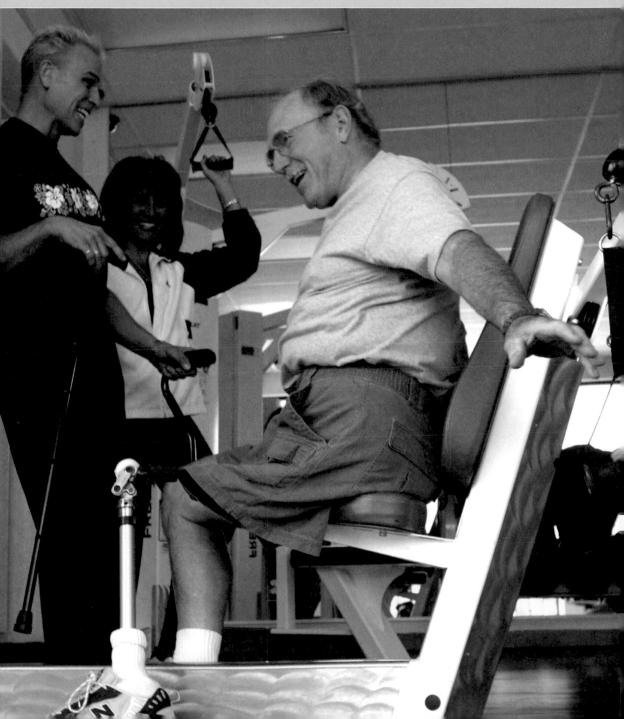

A Theater Director Confronts Throat Cancer

John Dillon

John Dillon is the director of the theater program at Sarah Lawrence College and has directed plays at theaters around the world. He is also a survivor of throat cancer. Dillon was diagnosed with stage-four cancer, which is cancer's most advanced stage. He describes his surgery and six weeks of radiation therapy. Dillon's approach to coping with the ordeal was unique. Because of his background in the theater, Dillon chose to dramatize the experience. He describes how he pictured himself as a cancer warrior. He scripted his treatment, casting family, friends, and colleagues in silly roles. His positive attitude has had its payoff. Dillon is a seven-year survivor.

Photo on previous page. After losing his leg to cancer, Bill Rudolph remained active and graduated from the Cancer Well Fit Program at the Santa Barbara Athletic Club in California. **(AP Images)**

A few years back I was diagnosed with throat cancer, and I was forced to confront my little homily on art's applicability to everyday life in ways I'd never imagined.

SOURCE: John Dillon, "Staging Cancer: Facing the Ordeal of His Life, a Director Embraces All Things Theatrical," *American Theatre*, December 2002, p. 75. Copyright © 2002 Theatre Communications Group. All rights reserved. Reproduced by permission.

It was a stage-four squamous-cell carcinoma, to be more precise (there is no stage five), and I remember thinking at the moment the doctor gave me my diagnosis: Here it is, perhaps the most dramatic moment in my life, and it's utterly untheatrical (but then I had yet to meet Maggie Edson or direct her powerful drama, *Wit*). And then, without realizing what I was doing, I began to theatricalize my cancer treatment, creating a script, working through a design process, casting my drama and then staging it.

The "easy" part, much to my astonishment, was the surgery to remove the malignant lymph nodes on the left side of my throat—four hours under the knife that meant permanently removing part of my jugular vein (the cancer had wrapped itself around it), removing the main left neck muscle (the sternocleidomastoid) as well as severing most of the sensory nerves in my neck (my Svengali surgeon, Ernie Weymuller, also painstakingly dissected my tongue's nerves from the tumor). After a few miserable days in the hospital, I was home and mending quickly, downing vast quantities of hot fudge sundaes and double cheeseburgers as I bulked up for the main event: head and neck radiation. The primary tumor was in an inoperable place on the base of my tongue, and only a six-week course of radiation would offer the hope of killing it. The problem was that going under the "big beam" would also kill most everything else in the area: saliva glands, hair follicles and almost every atom of the throat lining that allows us to swallow. In other words, with my throat lining about to be burnt off, I was about to experience the mother of all sore throats; and if I wanted to make a more rapid and complete recovery, I had to keep my weight up. I'd have to swallow, no matter the pain.

Fantasies Helped Ease the Pain

I figured the only way to get through this was to devise a scenario to play in my mind as I underwent radiation.

Otherwise I was left with images from one insensitive specialist's description: "We call this dropping the A-bomb on it." To my great good fortune, one of the doctors sharing the offices with my terrific general practitioner was skilled in "imaging," in helping patients free-associate as they developed "scripts" that placed treatment in a more positive light. We set up several long sessions to develop my scenario. But, thanks to a 30-year career in the theatre, and much to the doctor's surprise, we finished the whole process in less than three-quarters of an hour in our initial session.

My idea was this: It was my choice to undergo treatment for my cancer, so I would use that idea to empower myself each time I lay down on the treatment table and the beam was positioned to start zapping me with rads. As it was explained to me, radiation therapy is the attempt to administer an almost lethal dose of radiation. Healthy (and slower-growing) cells will eventually recover, but not the faster-growing malignant ones. I didn't want to focus on the "ordeal" aspect—I wanted a more positive image. So I created a story involving a Caribbean island and six special people on the beach—but more of that in a bit.

First I Had to Be Fitted for My Mask

The slightest head movement during treatment could send radiation into the spine instead of its intended target in the neck, possibly resulting in paralysis, so I was fitted with a plastic mesh mask exactly fitted to my face, with openings for my eyes. In the treatment room, I'd lie down on a suspended slab, hold two ropes attached to a board underneath my feet to keep my arms and shoulders down and still, while my head and mask were bolted down to the table. The rest of the staff checked my tattoos (yes, they gave me three tiny ones on my neck) to make sure I was lined up right for treatment. Then a linear accelerator swung over my head, underneath it and on both sides to deliver the treatment. The first thing I decided was that this wasn't a mask at all (I wasn't hiding: I'd chosen to undergo the treatment) but my helmet, just the fashion accessory needed for my new profession: cancer warrior. Within days of starting treatment, the team in the radiation oncology staff had joined in with my effort, now calling the mask my helmet. (After therapy was done, it was offered to me as a memento, and someone suggested turning it into topiary, but I didn't have the heart.)

As you might imagine, the treatment room itself could be forbidding, with its medical paraphernalia and a

Cancer patient T.J. Dreveniak is prepared for radiation therapy on his brain tumor. Like John Dillon, he has been fitted with a plastic mask that will hold his head perfectly still and ensure the radiation is directed at the correct spot. **(AP Images)**

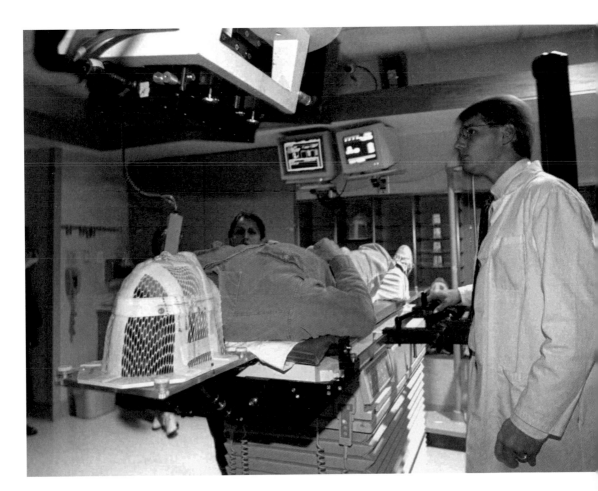

FAST FACT

According to the American Dental Association, chemicals found in tobacco cause 75 percent of all cancers of the mouth, throat, tongue, and lips.

2,000-pound, lead-lined door to protect the staff outside as they maneuvered and fired the "beam." I needed to convert the set into something a bit more benign. I remembered something that, I believe, Stacy Keach once said in an interview on film acting. Rather than trying to ignore the omnipresent camera, he'd give it a nickname and greet it each morning. So, on the first day of treatment, I asked if the accelerator had a nickname. Someone recalled it used to be called "Hillary" even before the Clintons were in the White House, so Hillary it was, and each day in the treatment room began with greeting Hillary and asking what she'd been up to. But I needed something more to combat the antiseptic nuclear environment of the treatment chamber—and that proved to be: costume design to the rescue.

Support Comes from Friends

Friends had been asking what they could do to help me during my bout with cancer. Taking inspiration from my life partner's lively footwear, I replied that healing prayers would be great, but if you wanted to do more, send me some silly socks. In they poured: socks festooned with funny animals, fruits, cartoons, masterworks of art, socks with brightly colored individual toes, and on and on. Each day I'd choose a different pair, and each day, as the beam got ready to start its four short bursts, I'd know something remarkably silly was on my feet, a reminder of all the friends out there wishing me well as my toes flouted the clinical atmosphere around me.

And it was during treatment that I most needed to stage my "script" in my mind. Rather than being subjected to near lethal doses of radiation, I told myself that I was really lying on a pristine Caribbean beach on a cloudy day. I had asked the oncology staff (saints all, and amateur hams, too, I suspect, for they always seemed to relish my theatrical ways of coping with treatment) to alert me when the beam was about to start its work. At that moment I would choose six friends and place them under some shady trees on the beach with me. On my signal, I'd imagine them gently lifting me up and, laughing and joking, carrying me into the warm ocean water. Then, with cries of "good luck" and "we love you," they'd all repair to the beach. As the beam began, I would imagine myself willing the clouds to part, and I'd ask the healing rays of sunlight to come down and rid me of the cancer on my tongue. I was trying to transform a deathly environment into a healing one and, just as important, I was imagining myself to be the one in control—a necessary antidote to the helplessness most of us cancer patients feel.

It was fun, too, casting my half-dozen co-stars each day. Sometimes I'd choose family members or neighbors. Sometimes I'd choose groups of friends by city (New York, Milwaukee, Tokyo, Los Angeles). One of my favorites was artistic directors. I'd been one myself for 16 years, and the ability to choose any six of my former colleagues and place them in outrageous swim gear on a beach was a hoot (well, amusements are sometimes limited for the ill, but I invite you to try the game when the pressures of looking for work get a bit much). . . .

Theatrics Helped Cure the Cancer

When my radiation therapy finally came to an end, Johanna and I wanted to thank the clinic's wonderful staff for all their care and their cooperation with my various cancer-coping strategies. Since "silly-sock therapy" had become something of a slogan around the clinic, Johanna had the inspired idea of buying the staff some outrageous footwear, each chosen to match the passions or the personality of the person. When we came back that afternoon for the final "dose" ("We've got one more cancer cell we're going to kill," as Dr. Cole put it), we realized that everyone on the staff, receptionists included, was wearing their silly socks in honor of my final "zap." We'd costumed the whole ward! After treatment (and the last imaginary gang of six swimwear-attired comrades) we all posed for joyous pictures, with skirts and pants hiked up to expose those silly socks.

I've wanted to write about how my battle with cancer was so greatly aided by the techniques I'd used all my adult life in my theatre work, but it seemed like tempting fate. But recently I returned to see Dr. Weymuller for my five-year checkup. "Clean as a whistle" was his verdict, and he told me I could consider myself cured. Theatre helped get me there.

What have I learned? That cancer may change our bodies, but we are the ones who can change who we really are. I've learned a greater appreciation for the tools I use as a theatre artist, and I recognize their deeper potential significance in living our lives with simultaneous clear-headedness and passionate creativity. What else? This little mantra: Cherish your friends. Treasure each day. Be useful.

Cancer Myths
and Truths

Caroline Bollinger, Sharon Liao, Maura Kelly, Julie D. Blumenfeld, and Amy Kamensky

In the following article a number of cancer survivors tell their stories. They portray the disease and its treatment as it really is, not how it is depicted in movies. These survivors have fought bone, uterine, breast, and bladder cancer, leukemia, and lymphoma. They reveal their fears and frustrations. They share experiences about friends who turn away from them.

I t's not always as bad as it seems. And sometimes, it's much, much worse.

Sixteen Survivors Reveal the Biggest Myths

We've all seen a movie of the week about a woman with cancer who survives against all odds and gets the cute

SOURCE: Caroline Bollinger, Sharon Liao, Maura Kelly, Julie D. Blumenfeld, and Amy Kamensky, "Everything You Know About Cancer Is Wrong," *Prevention*, November 2005. Copyright © 2005 Rodale, Inc. Reproduced by permission.

guy in the end. These stories have taught us that cancer bestows valuable lessons; that doctors always know what's best; that everyone comes together to support the heroine. Well, you'll be shocked—shocked—to discover that Hollywood doesn't always get it right. So we asked the people who really know: cancer survivors from all walks of life—celebrities, authors, athletes, doctors. We delivered the television bromides; they responded with the unvarnished truth.

Myth: Doctors Know Best

"The surgeon I went to initially said, 'You have so many questions. Why don't you read a book by a doctor named Susan Love? Then you won't have to annoy me.' That's a direct quote. I told him I would not only get her book —I'd ask her to do my surgery. And she did." —Linda Ellerbee, broadcast journalist, author, breast cancer survivor

"The worst piece of advice I ever got was, 'Just listen to your doctor and do what she tells you.' I needed to do my own research and talk to people who'd been through it." —Fran Visco, president of the National Breast Cancer Coalition, breast cancer survivor

"I was told I had 6 months to live, but after 2 years of treatment, my cancer went away, and it has never returned. It's been 15 years." —Kevin Sharp, country singer, bone cancer survivor

Myth: You'll Gain a Healthy Perspective on Life

"I thought cancer would automatically make me centered; that it would turn me into a saint; that immediately, I would get my priorities straight and stop sweating the small stuff. But pretty quickly, I realized that I was still stressing about work, fighting with my boyfriend, yelling at my sister." —Erin Zammett, author of My (So-Called) Normal Life, leukemia survivor

"I kept hearing that your attitude is the most important thing. When I had complications and my cancer returned, I kept thinking, Why can't I do this better? Is this my fault?" —Wendy Harpham, MD, author of *Happiness in a Storm: Facing Illness and Embracing Life as a Healthy Survivor*, non-Hodgkin's lymphoma survivor

Myth: You'll Never Be Afraid Again

"If you've had cancer, don't sleep alone! Get a pet if you don't have a mate. Sometimes you wake up in the middle of the night and your mind plays tricks on you. That's

A patient at the Nevada Cancer Institute in Las Vegas watches television while receiving her chemotherapy treatment. **(AP Images)**

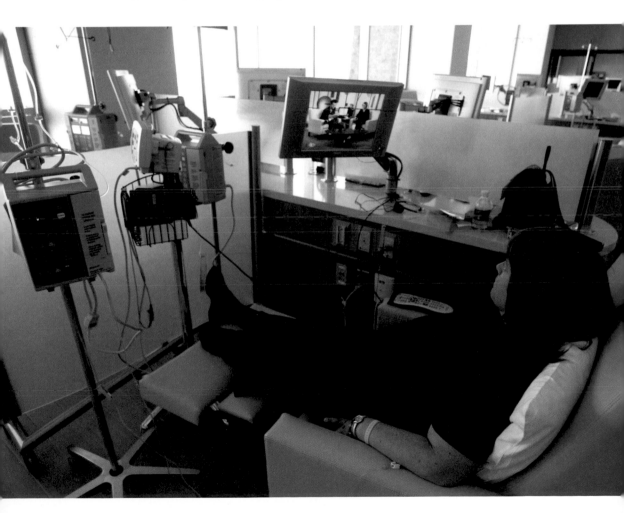

FAST FACT

According to the National Cancer Institute no conclusive evidence links underarm deodorants and antiperspirants with breast cancer in spite of stories in the press.

when you need something alive that you can hold on to." —Fran Drescher, actress, author, uterine cancer survivor

"Even after my treatment was finished, there was never a feeling that it was over. I kept waiting for the other shoe to drop." —Sandra Steingraber, PhD, author of *Living Downstream*, biologist, bladder cancer survivor

Myth: You Will be Damaged Goods

"Chemo was like an inside-out exfoliation. My skin is better; I don't break out anymore; my hair is thicker than it used to be. I actually feel better and healthier now." —Melissa Etheridge, musician, breast cancer survivor

"Cancer made me more in touch with my sexuality. Before, I never felt beautiful or that I was one of those people who deserved to wear lipstick. Finding out that I can have one boob, be balding and shedding, made me rethink what beauty is and what it means to be a woman." —Geralyn Lucas, author of *Why I Wore Lipstick to My Mastectomy*, breast cancer survivor

"After chemo, my hair came back in straight rather than curly, and I was ecstatic over that. My whole life I'd wanted straight hair!" —Sharon Osbourne, reality TV star, founder of the Sharon Osbourne Colon Cancer Foundation, colon cancer survivor

Myth: Cancer Brings People Closer Together

"A friend of mine said, 'You know, your friends don't want to hear about your disease. You need to go to a support group with other people who have cancer.'" —Sean Patrick, founder of HERA "Climb for Life" annual climb, ovarian cancer survivor

"You find out who your friends are. People either rally to support you or fall by the wayside."—Corina Morariu, professional tennis player, leukemia survivor

"A lot of well-meaning people told me how many people they knew who had died of breast cancer. That's not helpful." —Geralyn Lucas, author of *Why I Wore Lipstick to My Mastectomy*, breast cancer survivor

Myth: Treatment Will Be Terrible

"I quickly learned that chemo ruled my Fridays, but it didn't have to rule my life." —JoAnna Lund, coauthor of *When Life Hands You Lemons, Make Lemon Meringue Pie*, breast cancer survivor

"I thought chemotherapy was going to ravage my body, but I never felt very sick. At its worst, I had a really unpleasant taste in my mouth and was queasy the first day and a half after treatment." —Randi Rosenberg, president of the Young Survival Coalition, breast cancer survivor

Myth: Treatment Will Be a Piece of Cake

"I assumed I'd get skinny after chemo—that would be my silver lining. Instead I got fat! That didn't seem fair. And I still haven't lost the weight." —Cokie Roberts, political commentator for ABC News, breast cancer survivor

"I had a radical hysterectomy, an appendectomy, and I had about 50 lymph nodes removed. My doctors told me that I would be up and around, feeling fine in 6 weeks. Six months later, I still didn't feel like myself. I thought I was a failure. I thought, I am the worst patient!" —Fran Drescher, actress, author, uterine cancer survivor

Life Is Never the Same

"The difficult part of having cancer isn't the actual disease; it's figuring out what to do once you've survived. You have to go about living your life after it's been turned upside down." —Corina Morariu, professional tennis player, leukemia survivor

"The day before my diagnosis, I thought I was healthy, and the day after, I knew that I wasn't. There's a sense of loss for the rest of your life, knowing that your health is flawed." —David H. Johnson, MD, deputy director of Vanderbilt-Ingram Cancer Center, non-Hodgkin's lymphoma survivor

"After I started treatment, I seemed to be getting more cellulite and I asked my doctor, 'Could this be a side effect?' He was like, Well, uh . . . No.'" —Erin Zammett, author of *My (So-Called) Normal Life*, leukemia survivor

A Swimmer Fights Lung Cancer to the End

P.H. Mullen

P.H. Mullen has written a book about the swimmers of the U.S. Olympic team in 2000. In this article he relates the story of Jon Steiner, a swimmer who was fighting lung cancer. The disease, Mullen notes, is usually diagnosed late and then it spreads rapidly. He describes the onset of the disease in Steiner, who competed in the Masters World Championship. Even though the disease was in an advanced stage and had weakened him significantly, he completed the final leg of a men's 200-meter relay. It was, Mullen says, his last swim.

Jon Steiner didn't dive into the water because he was looking to inspire us.

Yet that's what he did. He managed it with just one lap. It was neither fast nor particularly pretty.

What it possessed, however, was more heart than an Olympic final.

SOURCE: P.H. Mullen, "Survive and Thrive: A Lesson in Living," *Swimming World*, April 2007, p. 30. Reprinted with express written consent of *Swimming World Magazine*, www.SwimmingWorld Magazine.com.

FAST FACT

According to a 2006 study, lung cancer is the leading cancer killer in both men and women in the U.S.

Were you there that sunny day last August [2006] at the FINA Masters World Championships? Were you among the fortunate who stood and cheered and wiped unexpected tears as a dying man gave us a lesson in how to live?

Steiner's race was the anchor leg of a 200 meter freestyle relay. It was magnificent. It was also a mighty struggle, for he was ravaged by lung cancer.

Lung Cancer Came Suddenly

His disease had arrived suddenly just months earlier, and it was devastating. His sturdy, bear-like body had become a gaunt comma. He needed assistance walking to his lane. He breathed on an oxygen tank until race time.

A man who can't breathe when he's sitting on land has no business trying to breathe in water.

Those 50 meters were a fight. It took forever. The other lanes emptied. The emotional crowd went crazy when he weakly touched the wall. Friends gently lifted him out.

His triumph that day is even more affecting in retrospect. Steiner died the following month at age 56.

His last swim got him a standing ovation.

Thriving to the End

With his trim beard, barrel chest and smiling eyes, Steiner knew how to thrive. He had a family and two daughters. By day, he was a successful lawyer. By night, he played jazz guitar professionally with his band, the Jon Steiner Trio.

And, of course, he loved to paddle back and forth.

He was never a top-10 swimmer, but he was a cornerstone of the Tamalpais Aquatic Masters (TAM) in San Rafael, Calif. He spent considerable time volunteering with local and national Masters committees. He was legal counsel for the 2006 FINA Masters Local Organizing Committee, and continued with the role as his health declined.

In spring 2006, he raced at Masters Nationals in Florida. Something was off. Despite a good taper, his times were much slower than a month earlier. But most troubling was his difficulty taking deep breaths. He went home to a doctor.

You don't see much lung cancer. It's difficult to catch early, and can spread with chilling speed. Usually, it kills quickly. A person gets sick, and doesn't recover. For all types of lung cancer at all stages, Cancer Research UK calculates one-year survivorship is just 20 percent.

Cancer Cannot Stop the Swimmer

Steiner's disease progressed rapidly. His swim club's spring 2006 newsletter wished him and others good luck

Frank Maloy, a lung cancer patient, prepares for radiation therapy at the M.D. Anderson Proton Therapy center in Houston. (**AP Images**)

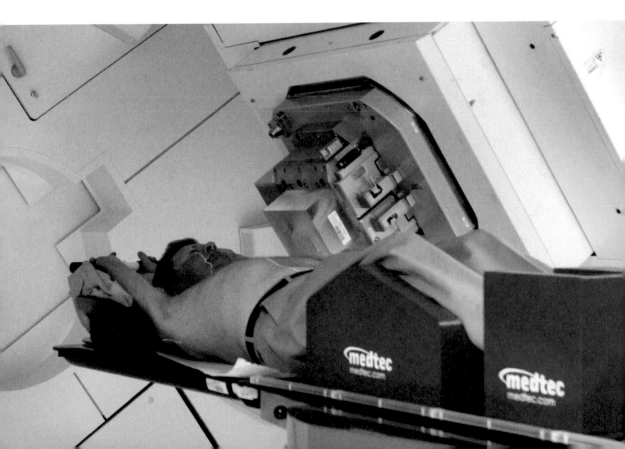

at nationals. The summer issue wished him a speedy recovery. The autumn edition announced a memorial fund-raising event renamed in his honor.

Friends say the sicker he grew, the more important swimming the Masters World Championships became to him. Before falling ill, he had entered individual events. Those had to be scratched. But his teammates rallied and set up a relay.

You could say his swim was folly, because it surely weakened his fragile system.

Or you could see it quite differently. You could say it was a brave act by someone who knew the odds were against him, but refused to give up his optimism.

Surviving and thriving occur at all moments of life, even final ones. In fact, a defining act of willful determination probably happens most often near the end of a person's life. Usually, it doesn't play in public.

We got lucky this time. We were able to be witnesses to a lesson in living.

Steiner showed us how to finish strong, even amid the fear and confusion.

That last swim—it was his gift to us.

Our gift back to him is to show that we understood it.

GLOSSARY

angiogenesis — The process of developing new blood vessels.

benign tumor — A noncancerous growth comprising cells that reproduce uncontrollably but do not spread to other tissues.

biopsy — Living tissue is surgically removed during this process to be microscopically examined for disease.

cancer — This disease involves a population of cells that grow and spread beyond the normal limits, damaging the body's normal cells and tissues.

carcinogen — Any substance capable of causing cancer by mutating a cell's DNA.

carcinoma — These cancers grow in the epithelium, the cells that cover the body's surface and line the internal organs and glands. Ninety percent of all cancers are carcinomas.

chemotherapy — Drugs used to destroy cancer cells. Chemotherapy selectively kills the cancer cells that have broken away from the primary tumor and have spread throughout the body.

clinical test — The procedure of testing a new drug for safety and effectiveness in treating a particular disease or condition. Clinical tests are carried out under strict controls to assure the most accurate results. The Food and Drug Administration makes its decision to approve a drug or not based on these tests.

complementary and alternative medicine (CAM) — Medical practices that fall outside the conventional treatments prescribed by doctors. CAMs are sometimes used in addition to prescribed medicine—to reduce pain, for example.

glioma — A cancer that attacks the nerve tissue, often in the brain or spinal cord.

hormone therapy   Cancer treatment that blocks the production of hormones that stimulate cancer growth. Breast cancer and prostate cancer are slowed by blocking estrogen and testosterone, respectively.

imaging tests   These tests help doctors locate a tumor even if it is deep in the body. These tests include Magnetic Resonance Imaging (MRI) and Computed Topography scans (CT Scans), among others.

immunotherapy   This cancer treatment stimulates substances already produced by the body's immune system to reject and destroy cancerous growths. This treatment is relatively new and not available for many types of cancer.

leukemia   Cancer of the blood or bone marrow characterized by a rise in immature white blood cell count and a drop in necessary red blood cell numbers.

lumpectomy   The surgical removal of breast tumors and minimal amounts of surrounding tissues.

lymphoma   Cancer that begins in the lymph glands of the immune system.

malignant   These tumor cells can spread to invade and destroy other tissues and organs.

mammography   The process of examining soft breast tissue with low-dose X-rays to find possible cysts or tumors.

mastectomy   The surgical removal of all breast tissue, in one or both breasts, in order to treat or prevent cancer.

melanoma   A particularly dangerous cancer found most commonly in the skin.

metastasis   The spread of cancerous cells from one part of the body to another, often through blood or lymphatic vessels.

mutation   Changes to DNA (deoxyribonucleic acid) of a cell, caused by mistakes during cell division or damage from environmental agents. Mutations can be harmful, beneficial, or insignificant. Some genetic mutations interfere with the regulation of cell division and can lead to cancer.

oncogene	A gene that directs cell growth. Altered oncogenes can transform normal cells into cancerous ones.
oncology	The branch of medicine that diagnoses and treats cancer.
Pap smear	A test in which cervical cells from a vaginal smear are stained and examined for abnormalities and cancer.
pathogen	A biological agent that causes disease, often cancer. For example, papillomaviruses lead to cancer of the cervix.
pathologist	A doctor who studies and diagnoses diseases by examining cells and tissues under a microscope.
primary tumor	The tumor where the cell mutation and uncontrollable growth begins.
prostatectomy	The surgical removal of part or all of the prostate gland for early stage cancer or for cancer that will not respond to radiation therapy.
radiation therapy	Treatment that uses radiation to kill cancer cells. Radiation therapy can be used in lieu of surgery to destroy a tumor or in conjunction with surgery and chemotherapy. Radiation can be externally applied or taken internally as pellets or liquid.
remission	State in which evidence and symptoms of cancer have decreased or disappeared. This state may be temporary or permanent.
sarcoma	Cancer of supporting tissues of the body, such as bone, muscle, and blood vessels.
secondary tumor	Tumors that grow after the cancer cells metastasize from the primary tumor. Secondary tumors can appear in any part of the body and do not need to be near the primary tumor.
stages	The extent of one's cancer is classified into one of four stages. Stage I cancer is confined to a primary tumor. Stages II and III vary according to the type of cancer, but are generally confined to the primary cancer and nearby lymph nodes. Stage IV cancer is advanced and metastasized, and it is considered inoperable.

CHRONOLOGY

B.C. **400** Hippocrates first describes malignant tumors as *carcinos* (Greek for "crab") to distinguish them from benign tumors. He later added the -oma suffix (Greek for "swelling") to create the term *carcinoma*.

A.D. **1761** English doctor John Hill discovers the relationship between nasal tobacco and cancer.

1858 Rudolf Virchow, a German pathologist, develops the theory that each cell originates from another existing cell. This theory will be an important guide for later cancer research to focus attention on the origins of cancer cells.

1913 The American Society for the Control of Cancer is founded. It is renamed the American Cancer Society in 1945.

1914 Theodor Boveri, a German biologist, develops the theory that cancer is genetically based.

1924 Cancer surpasses tuberculosis as a cause of death in America.

1934 Cancer becomes the number two cause of death in America, second only to heart disease.

1942 Wilhelm Hueper publishes *Occupational Tumors and Allied Diseases,* the first comprehensive classification of cancerous damage caused by industrial chemicals.

1946 The American Cancer Society promotes the widespread use of the Pap smear to detect cervical and uterine cancer.

1950 Research linking smoking to cancer is published.

1954 The Tobacco Research Committee (TRC) is formed by major American manufacturers of cigarettes. The committee publishes reports indicating that there is no conclusive link between cancer and smoking.

1955 Charles Huggins researches the connections between hormones and cancer. He determines that testosterone fuels the growth of prostate cancer and estrogen fuels the growth of breast cancer.

1961 Angiogenesis (the process by which a network of blood vessels feed oxygen to a tumor) is discovered by Judah Folkman of Harvard University.

1971 President Richard M. Nixon signs the National Cancer Act, which establishes a national program to find a cure for cancer.

1978 The Food and Drug Administration (FDA) approves Tamoxifen, a drug that blocks estrogen receptors on cancer cells, to treat breast cancer.

1980 The Bristol Cancer Help Center opens, offering cancer patients a range of alternative therapies.

1986   The FDA approves the prostate-specific antigen (PSA) test to screen men for prostate cancer.

1990   Cancer prevention trials data show that eating fruits and vegetables lowers the risk of contracting colon cancer.

1992   The FDA approves Taxol, a compound from the bark of the Pacific yew tree, to treat ovarian cancer. It also proves useful in treating breast and lung cancers.

1996   The American Cancer Society's *Guidelines on Diet, Nutrition, and Cancer* state that one-third of all cancer deaths could be avoided by regular exercise and eating right.

1996   Cancer prevention studies prove that nonsmoking spouses of smokers have an increased risk of lung cancer and heart disease.

2004   Scientists discover a blood test to screen for colon cancer. In the same year the FDA approves the use of Erbitux and Avastin to treat colon cancer.

2006   The FDA approves Gardasil, a vaccine that protects against the human papillomavirus that causes the most incidences of cervical cancer.

ORGANIZATIONS TO CONTACT

The editors have compiled the following list of organizations concerned with the issues debated in this book. The descriptions are derived from materials provided by the organizations. All have publications or information available for interested readers. The list was compiled on the date of publication of the present volume; the information provided here may change. Be aware that many organizations take several weeks or longer to respond to inquiries, so allow as much time as possible.

American Cancer Society
1599 Clifton Rd.
Atlanta, GA 30329
(800) 227-2345
www.cancer.org

The American Cancer Society (ACS) is a national organization with over 3,400 local offices. The ACS provides information, supports community services, funds research and acts as an advocacy group to the government. The Web site offers information about treatment and care and resource information for cancer patients and their families.

American Institute for Cancer Research
1759 R St. NW
Washington, DC 20009
(800) 843-8114
www.aicr.org

The American Institute for Cancer Research (AICR) was established in 1982 and works to educate the public about the links between diet and cancer. The organization funds research related to diet and cancer prevention, as well as other research studies. The AICR publishes pamphlets, newsletters, and other materials.

Association of Cancer Online Resources
173 Duane St., Suite 3A
New York, NY 10013-3334
(212) 226-5525
www.acor.org

The Association of Cancer Online Resources was one of the first social networking sites. The Web site allows for information sharing among patients, caregivers, and health professionals. The Web site offers a variety of features including offering basic information on various types of cancer, as well as links to other resources, and bibliography lists for further research.

Cancer Research Institute
One Exchange Plaza
55 Broadway,
Suite 1802
New York, NY 10006
(800) 992-2623
www.cancer
research.org

The Cancer Research Institute is a fifty-year-old organization that supports cancer research around the world. The Web site includes publications about surviving cancer and research conducted.

Centers for Disease Control and Prevention
Division of Cancer Prevention and Control
4770 Buford Hwy.,
NE MS K-64
Atlanta, GA 30341
(888) 232-6348
www.cdc.gov/cancer

The Centers for Disease Control and Prevention (CDC) work with cancer organizations and health agencies to develop, implement, and promote effective strategies for the prevention and control of cancer. The Web site provides information on screening, medical research, and further resources.

Lance Armstrong Foundation
PO Box 161150
Austin, TX 78716
(512) 236-8820
www.livestrong.org

Founded by cancer survivor and world-class cyclist Lance Armstrong, the foundation provides financial support for cancer research and direct support for cancer survivors. The Web site has educational information and downloadable publications.

M.D. Anderson Cancer Center
The University of Texas
1515 Holcombe Blvd.
Houston, TX 77030
(800) 392-1611
www.mdanderson.org

M.D. Anderson Cancer Center's Web site provides information about the services offered to its cancer patients, survivors' stories, general cancer information, and a free online newsletter.

Memorial Sloan-Kettering Cancer Center
1275 York Ave.
New York, NY 10021
(212) 639-2000
www.mskcc.org

The Web site of Memorial Sloan-Kettering Cancer Center includes information about the full range of cancers, research that is being undertaken at the center and other locations, and opportunities for students and medical professionals at the center.

National Breast Cancer Foundation, Inc.
2600 Network Blvd., Suite 300
Frisco, Texas 75034
www.national breastcancer.org

The National Breast Cancer Foundation is dedicated to saving lives through awareness, education, and support. The foundation provides free mammograms in attempts to catch and treat breast cancer early. The Web site provides a library of informative articles and the opportunity to participate in group discussions.

National Cancer Institute
6116 Executive Blvd., Room 3036A
Bethesda, MD 20892
(800) 422-6237
www.cancer.gov

The National Cancer Institute, a branch of the federal government, offers information on specific cancers as well as a help line and online chat service. The Web site contains research information and statistics for both the public and the medical community.

Prostate Cancer Research Institute
5777 West Century Blvd., Suite 800
Los Angeles, CA 90045
(310) 743-2116
www.prostate-cancer.org

The Prostate Cancer Research Institute was founded by oncologists and prostate cancer specialists in order to educate patients and their families about prostate cancer. On the Web site can be found information on advances, staging, and resources, encouraging patients to be well-informed so they can receive the best care possible.

St. Jude Children's Research Hospital
332 N. Lauderdale
Memphis, TN 38105
(901) 495-3300
www.stjude.org

St. Jude Children's Research Hospital is the nation's third largest health care charity, treating children with cancer and other catastrophic diseases. The Web site shares information about the research being done at St. Jude and the resources available to cancer patients and their families.

FOR FURTHER READING

Books

Greg Anderson, *Cancer: 50 Essential Things to Do*. New York: Plume (Penguin), 1999.

C. Norman Coleman, *Understanding Cancer: A Patient's Guide to Diagnosis, Prognosis, and Treatment*. Baltimore, MD: Johns Hopkins University Press, 2006.

Malin Dollinger, Margaret Tempero, Earnest Rosenbaum, and Sean Mulvihill, *Everyone's Guide to Cancer Therapy*. 4th ed. Kansas City, MO: Andrews McMeel, 2002.

Harmon J. Eyre, *Informed Decisions: The Complete Book of Cancer Diagnosis, Treatment, and Recovery*. Atlanta, GA: American Cancer Society, 2002.

Jimmie Holland and Sheldon Lewis, *The Human Side of Cancer: Living with Hope, Coping with Uncertainty*. New York: Harper-Collins, 2000.

Rosanne Kalik, *Cancer Etiquette: What to Say, What to Do, When Someone You Know or Love Has Cancer*. Scarsdale, NY: Lion, 2004.

Michael L. Krychman, *100 Questions and Answers for Women Living with Cancer: A Practical Guide for Survivorship*. Sudbury, MA: Jones and Bartlett, 2007.

John Link, *Breast Cancer Survival Manual*. 4th ed. New York: Owl (Henry Holt), 2007.

Richard B. Patt, *The Complete Guide to Relieving Cancer Pain and Suffering*. New York: Oxford University Press, 2004.

Verne Verona, *Nature's Cancer Fighting Foods*. New York: Reward (Penguin Putnam), 2001.

Periodicals

Catherine Arnst, "Teaching the Body to Fix Itself," *Business Week*, April 30, 2007.

Patrick L. Barry, "Taking Cancer's Fingerprint," *Science News*, February 17, 2007.

Jack Challem, "Lycopene: The Tomato's Secret Weapon," *Better Nutrition*, March 2007.

Cortlandt Forum, "The Price of Curbing Cancer," November 2006.

Dermatology Nursing, "Skin Cancer Prevention," August 2006.

Economist, "Choose Your Poison," October 2006.

Brenda S. Halls and Peggy Ward Smith, "Identifying Early Symptoms of Pancreatic Cancer," *Clinical Journal of Oncology Nursing*, April 2007.

Harvard Men's Health Watch, "Obesity and Prostate Cancer," January 2007.

Michael Kalen, "Life Insurance Getting Much Easier for Cancer Survivors to Obtain," *National Underwriter/Life & Health Financial Services*, July 31, 2006.

Robin M. Lally, "Caring for Kids with Cancer Takes Passion, Conviction, and Commitment," *ONS News*, July 2006.

Massage & Bodywork, "Adolescent Use of CAM," December/January 2007.

Ralph W. Moss, "The War on Cancer," *Townsend Letter for Doctors and Patients*, November 2006.

Alison Motlik, "How Common Viruses Can Turn Cells Cancerous," *New Scientist*, March 2007.

Maryann Napoli, "How Prevalent Is Cancer? How Prevalent Are Cancers That Will Not Kill?" *Health Facts*, August 2006.

Newsweek, "What Breast Cancer Survivors Can Expect," April 2, 2007.

Alice Park, "Hormone Therapy Redeemed," *Time*, April 16, 2007.

Michael E. Pichichero, "Who Should Get the HPV Vaccine?" *Journal of Family Practice*, March 2007.

Zoltan P. Rona, "Cancer Prevention Checklist, *Canadian Journal of Health & Nutrition*, April 2007.

Phil Sneiderman, "Aid in Predicting Cancer Cases," *CongressDaily*, February 15, 2007.

Liz Szabo, "Prices Soar for Cancer Drugs," *Gerson Healing Newsletter*, September/October 2006.

Robert Ullman and Judyth Reichenberg–Ullman, "Healing with Homeopathy," *Townsend Letter for Doctors and Patients*, August/September 2006.

Marcella Williams, "Gynecologic Cancers," *Clinical Journal of Oncology Nursing*, April 2007.

Hillary Wright, "Getting Physically Active May Increase Your Chances of Surviving Cancer," *Environmental Nutrition*, March 2007.

INDEX

A

Abrams, Donald, 94

Acupuncture, 77

Adams, Heidi, 26

Adenocarcinomas, 15

Adolescents/young adults, 21

Advisory Committee of Immunization
Practices (ACIP), 66, 67, 71

Aging, 7, 9

Albritton, Karen, 24

Alternative treatments
for cancer are effective, 76–83
for cancer do not work, 84–88

Altieri, Dario, 40

American Cancer Society, 58

Antioxidants, 77–79, 85–86

Apoptosis, 39

B

Benson, John, 91

Bleyer, Archie, 23

Bone cancer, 24

Breast cancer
incidence/mortality ratio of, 28
research, 27–31
in younger women, 23

Burke, Megan, 25

C

Calcium, 80

Cancer(s)
alternative treatments
are effective, 76–83
do not work, 84–88
among young people, 20–26
caused by infections, 75
characteristics of, 12
diagnoses/deaths from, 13
in elderly, 8–10
gene therapy, 32–37
incidence of, 21
lifetime risk for, 18
risk factors/warning signs of, 16
survivors' narratives on, 109–114
types of, 15
See also specific types

Cancer cells, 39, 40

Carcinomas, 15

Cells, 25

Centers for Disease Control and
Prevention (CDC), 65, 71

Ceravix, 66

Cervical cancer
incidence of, 67
vaccine against, 70–75
as effective, 64–69

Chemotherapy
marijuana and, 89–95
risk for bone cancer, 24

Clarke, Paul, 41

Craker, Lyle, 92–93

D
Deaths. *See* Mortality/mortality rates
Diagnosis, 16–17
 delays in, 8
Dichloroacetate (DCA), 38–41
Diet
 in prevention of cancer, 76–77
 See also Lifestyle behaviors
DNA, 13, 34, 77
 mutations in, 15, 30
 progress in analysis of, 29
Drescher, Fran, 112, 113
Drug Enforcement Administration
 (DEA), 92–94
drug trials
 of Gardasil, 66, 73–75
 for gene therapy, 36
 lack of young adults in, 23

E
Eliaz, Isaac, 77, 82
Ellerbee, Linda, 110
Environmental Protection Agency
 (EPA), 56
Equol, 81–82
Etheridge, Melissa, 112

F
Fisher, Barbara Loe, 71

G
Gardasil, 66, 71
Genes
 cancer as disease of, 13–15

 therapy with, 32-37
Genetics, breast cancer, 27–28
Genistein, 82
Gliomas, 15
Glycolysis, 39, 40
Guy, Geoffrey, 95

H
Hahn, Karin, 23
Harpham, Wendy, 111
Hayes-Lattin, Brandon, 21
*The Health Consequences of Involuntary
 Smoking* (U.S. Surgeon General), 48
Heart disease, 51–52
Human papillomavirus (HPV)
 abnormal Pap tests related to, 69
 incidence of, 65
 infection, 74
 vaccine against, 66–67, 73–75
Hunter, David, 29

I
Institute of Medicine (IOM), 90–91

J
Johnson, David H., 114

L
Lance Armstrong Foundation, 21
Leukemias, 51
Lifestyle behaviors
 as factors in cancers, 7
 leading to colorectal cancer, 77
 percent of cancers prevented by, 66
 to prevent prostate cancer, 46
 in prevention of cancer, 19, 83

Lifetime risk, 18
Liu, Jianjun, 28
Lucas, Geralyn, 112, 113
Lund, JoAnna, 113
Lung cancer, 7
    secondhand smoke as cause,
        48–54
    may not cause, 55–63
Lycopene, 79
Lymphomas, 15

M
Marijuana
    Chemotherapy and, 89–95
    has no medical application,
        96–100
    medical use for, 93, 95
Marinol, 91–92, 98
Medicines, 87
Melanoma, 7, 15
    annual deaths from, 37
    gene therapy for, 33
Men
    prostate cancer and, 42–46
    risk of cancer for, 18
Michelakis, Evangelos, 39
Mitochondria, 39
Modified Citrus Pectin (MCP), 82
Morariu, Corina, 113
Mortality/mortality rates
    annual cancer-related, 14
    in breast cancer, 28
    cancer-related
        aging and, 9
        as percent of global deaths, 18
    from prostate cancer, 43

Multiple Risk Factor Intervention
    Trial, 86
Mushrooms, medicinal, 83–84

N
National Cancer Institute, 7
National Cancer Institute (NCI), 21
National Collegiate Cancer Foundation,
    24

O
Oakland Cannabis Buyers Coop.,
    U.S. v., 98
Origer, Mark, 32, 34, 37
Osbourne, Sharon, 112

P
Papanicolaou (Pap) test, 68, 69
Patrick, Sean, 112
Prevention,
    genetic testing in, 34
    lifestyle behaviors and, 19, 83
    web sites for information on, 78
Prostate cancer, 42–46
    alternative therapies for, 81–82
    incidence of, 43

R
Rabin, Roni, 74–75
Research
    on medicinal marijuana, 92–94
    on new cancer therapies, 17
Roberts, Cokie, 113
Rodewald, Lance, 68
Rosenberg, Randi, 113
Rosenberg, Steven, 33, 35, 37

S
Sarcomas, 15
Sativex, 95
Schuchat, Anne, 66
Screening
  breast cancer, 29
  for prostate cancer, 42, 43
Secondhand smoke
  causes lung cancer, 48–54
  chemicals in, 50
  exposure to, 59
  may not cause cancer, 55–63
  See also Secondhand smoke
Selenium, 80
Sharp, Kevin, 110
Side effects
  of alternative medicines, 87
  of chemotherapy, 89–95
  of prostate cancer treatment, 45–46
smoking, 60–61, 63
Soy protein, 81–82
Squamous cell carcinomas, 15
Steiner, Jon, 115–118
Steingraber, Sandra, 112
Survival rates, 18–19
  of prostate cancer, 44
  of young cancer patients, 22–23

T
Tea, 80
THC (delta-9-tetrahydrocannabinol), 91, 92
Throat cancer, 102–108, 115–118
Treatment
  aims of, 17–18

delays in, 8
for marijuana abuse vs. other drugs, 99–100
for prostate cancer, 44–45
types of, 18
See also Alternative treatments
Tumors, 14–15

U
Ulman, Doug, 23–24
U.S. Food and Drug Administration, U.S. (FDA), 97
  on smoked marijuana, 90
U.S. v. Oakland Cannabis Buyers Coop., 98

V
Vaccine
  against cervical cancer, 64-69 70–75
Verma, Anjuli, 93
Visco, Fran, 110
Vitamins, 79–80, 87

W
Waeger, Dan, 24
Web sites, 78
White cells, 33
Women, 18
World Health Organization (WHO), 31, 66

Y
Youth. *See* Adolescents/young adults

Z
Zammett, Erin, 110, 114